BACKPACKING
for
Fun & Fitness

by
Clayne R. Jensen and Craig Jensen

Brigham Young University   University of Utah

Leisure Press
P.O. Box 3
West Point, N.Y. 10996

A publication of Leisure Press.
P.O. Box 3, West Point, N.Y. 10996
Copyright ©1981 Leisure Press
All rights reserved. Printed in the U.S.A.

(ISBN 0-918438-77-2)
1st Printing: August, 1981

Front cover photo: David Madison
Back cover photo: Skip Jones
Cover design: Diana Goodin

CONTENTS

PREFACE

Backpacking, an increasingly popular form of outdoor recreation, can be a truly rewarding experience. It offers safe, inexpensive enjoyment in a world of beauty and solitude. Depending upon your mood, you can strike out alone on a short trip, travel with congenial friends, or make it a family affair. Backpacking techniques are easy to learn, and you don't need fashionable clothing or expensive equipment.

Written especially for the thousands who want to go to the back country for adventure and enjoyment, this book includes many useful ideas and easy-to-apply skills which can contribute to the pleasure and safety of every outdoor enthusiast. The content was developed with clarity and practicality in mind and it has the prospect of opening up a whole new world of challenge and adventure for you. Backpacking might be exactly what is needed to add diversion and new dimension to your life.

Perhaps you are interested in hiking to a better fishing spot in Wisconsin or on the Snake River in Wyoming. Maybe you are a camera enthusiast with a burning desire to photograph wildlife in the Rockies, the Cascades or the Appalachians. Or you might be looking for a new kind of ruggedness in a desert of the great southwest. But probably you are like thousands of others who flood to the outdoors just to enjoy the beauty and serenity of the back country. So enjoy!

There is something to be said about shouldering your own pack and separating yourself from roads, televisions, telephones, and masses of people.

1
Reasons for Backpacking

Climb the mountains and get their good tidings. The winds will blow their freshness into you and the storms, their energy. Your cares and tensions will drop away like the leaves of autumn.
—John Muir

There is something positive to be said about shouldering your own pack and separating yourself from roads, televisions, telephones, and masses of people; where the importance of the clock gives way to the rhythm and cadence of nature. The person with the pack is not restrained; he goes where he wants and stops when he wants. He's there in the early morning and the late evening when nature is the most active, and he is constantly faced with the interesting challenge of blending himself with the environment. The backpacker's world embodies things not found elsewhere—not only the scenery, the mountain breeze and the open space, but also history, primitive experiences, and elements capable of lifting the spirit.

Aside from the American Indian, the earliest backpackers of this country were the frontiersmen who roamed the hills looking for fur animals and adventure during the country's formative years. For them, however, it was

7

necessity more than sport. Other early backpackers were the prospectors who packed heavy loads over mountains and across deserts in search of treasure. Backpacking always has played an important role in exploration of unknown territories.

Some areas such as snow covered slopes, heavily wooded terrain, and the Alaskan tundra are still inaccessible except by foot and pack. Also, the number of scenic and wilderness areas where travel into the back country is largely restricted to hiking is virtually inexhaustible.

For the highly enthusiastic, backpacking has no seasons—it can be enjoyed the year round; spring, summer, fall, and winter. Also, being one of the few activities that has appeal to all ages, backpacking can be a family sport.

Many of today's ecology minded youth take up backpacking in order to learn more about that which already interests them—nature. The activity can cause a pleasurable reuniting of people with the natural envitonment. It can both develop and satisfy the hidden pioneer spirit, because it offers the potential of going where no other person has been.

Backpacking in scenic country can be a renewing experience—a refreshing change from the work-a-day world and the domestic routine. It takes a person into areas that serve as laboratories for learning, museums for study, and playgrounds for wholesome enjoyment. It can afford people of all ages a special kind of fulfillment not available in unnatural settings. Backpacking affords each individual the opportunity to have his own rendezvous with the land, where he can develop special respect for the fundamental values of nature and pay particular attention to the way these relate to the good of people and society.

Some Practical Reasons

Backpacking is included in the programs of many youth agencies and educational programs for the purposes of (a) teaching practical outdoor skills, (b) preparing youth to handle themselves under stressful conditions, and (c) teaching them to make correct judgements in real life situations. Also, under good leadership, outdoor activities can build character, and the skills that are learned can contribute to one's qualifications as a survivor in emergency situations.

To photograph a natural scene one must go there with camera in hand, and the possibilities for dramatic and unique shots seem unlimited. Both professionals and amateurs have recognized this, and many take advantage of it in conjunction with their backpacking interests.

Some have found the study of wildlife in its natural habitat to their liking. Direct contact with nature, especially the living things in their native environment, can add immensely to one's appreciation and understanding of life.

For the hunter or fisherman who must go where the quarry is abundant, backpacking is more than a pleasant outing. It's a necessity, and a means to an end. It is certain that a fishing or hunting spot accessible only by a long backpacking trek will be less crowded than most others.

Some people still go backpacking in connection with their occupations. There are still professional trappers who backpack regularly, and many employees of the U.S. Forest Service, National Park Service, Soil Conservation Service, Fish and Wildlife Service, and U.S. Geological Survey, who find backpacking skills important in their work. Other interests can grow out of backpacking experiences, such as winter camping, river running and rock climbing.

Backpacking is a physical challenge to many—a test of stamina and skill. Fitness specialists agree that walking is one of the best activities for all ages. It's even better with a pack. Further, walking through areas that are attractive and interesting is better than doing four laps around the neighborhood block. People today need to design active lifestyles to keep their weight controlled and their body systems well conditioned. Jogging, cycling, skiing, and other active outdoor sports have mushroomed largely because people have awakened to the fact that the body must be exercised if an acceptable level of fitness is to be maintained. Most of those who participate regularly in backpacking are much better conditioned than they would be otherwise. It's important to prepare yourself for the stress and strain of a backpacking trip and then use judgment as to how far and how fast you travel.

For the hunter or fisherman who must go where the quarry is abundant, backpacking is more than a pleasant outing.

Some Precautions

The first ingredient of a safe and pleasant trip is **good planning**. The plan should include your destination, time schedule, who will go, food, clothing, sleeping equipment, shelter, fire and cooking arrangements, permits needed, and a plan for potential emergencies. Before each outing it would be well to review the contents of this book, which categorize the important information, and pay particular attention to the list of equipment found and the extras.

Carry a small **survival kit**—it could save your life. Leave a **trip schedule**, preferably in writing, with a responsible person giving the following information:

- Who is going and where.
- When you will leave and when you plan to return.
- A description of the vehicle you will use.
- Location of the trail head and the routes you expect to follow.

Above all, do not stay an extra day or two without notifying the appropriate persons. Search parties cost money and time.

Don't be too hasty about **buying equipment**. First talk to some experienced backpackers, and also do some experimentation of your own. Before buying, ask yourself "is it durable, reasonably light and compact, useful, and priced right?" Remember there is very little room for compromise of quality, because in the back country there are no stores or repair shops.

Environmental Considerations

In view of the heavy use that the out-of-doors receives and the escalation of use that will develop in the future, it is important to be highly considerate of the environment even in the most isolated wilderness areas. Practice "minimum impact camping." Here are some guidelines:

- Trees and shrubs grow slowly and are replaceable only over a long period. They need to be conserved and for this reason backpackers should avoid cutting them except in extreme emergency.
- Trash should always be carried out, not buried, because animals might dig it up and scatter it. This is the least we can do for those who follow.
- When you break camp, disassemble all materials that have been arranged for camping purposes.
- Be very conservative about building campfires and, if you do build one, drown it with water and scatter the ashes.
- Remember that in water drainage areas, trash and human waste have a contaminating effect, so they ought to be kept at least 100 yards from streams and lakes. Never pollute open water.
- Disturb wildlife and wildlife habitat as little as possible. Remember you're the visitor in their environment.

Figure 1-1. Full pack with sleeping bag attached. An example of a good job of packing, and a pack that is well placed on the body.

• Obtain the required permits and follow the regulations prescribed for the particular area.

• A good motto is "leave nothing but tracks and take nothing but photographs."

2
Characteristics of Modern Backpacks

The only way really to know a wilderness is to spend ample time in its native haunt, to study thoroughly its grandeur and beauty.

The human body is not well structured to carry heavy loads on the back, but through advances in backpack design over recent years, it has become possible for a person to carry a load of 30-50 pounds over a considerable distance with a fair amount of comfort. The art of developing the greatly improved features of the modern pack began in the 1950's. Prior to that time, rather crudely constructed and poorly designed packs were the rule.

Although the Kelty Company led the way in the design and construction of backpacks, numerous other manufacturers soon became involved. New features were developed such as the lightweight hipload frame, highly durable waterproof fabric, self sealing nylon zippers, and padded shoulder and belt straps. Recently, internal frame packs have emerged as a popular style. There is now a great variety of packs manufactured by more than fifty companies in the United States plus some that are imported from the Orient and Europe. They come in a variety of styles and sizes, some especially designed for the heavy load and others for ski touring, mountain and rock climbing, or one-day trips.

Packs range in price from less than $10 for small lightweight packs to more than $200 for large, top-quality packs. Anyone planning to do extensive backpacking ought to invest in at least a medium priced, brand-name back. Cheaply constructed packs are poor investments because they will not hold up under extensive use.

The most important considerations are **durability, fit** and **balance.** The size and features of the pack should conform to the kind of use it will receive and the size and shape of your body. Every individual is built differently—different front to back dimensions, different shoulder to hip distance, different alignment and center of gravity. All of these influence which pack is best for you. Also, the size of the pack is a consideration. As a general guide, a backpacker in good condition should carry no more than 25 percent of body weight.

Before purchasing a pack, determine the uses you will make of it, and therefore, what is needed in a pack to suit your purpose. Check thoroughly for proper fit, waterproofing, sturdy frame with no flaws, solid seams, and properly functioning zippers. If the pack is not sound in all important aspects, don't buy it. Purchasing from a sales person who is an experienced packer himself can be a great advantage. He can use his own experience in helping you decide the items of equipment that will best suit you and your purpose. Also, it is advisable to shop at a store that carries a variety of high quality backpacking equipment.

The Pack Frame

Many modern backpacks consist of a frame, and a pack which is attached to the frame in some manner. These two components, properly fitted, can provide comfort while carrying a heavy load. The frame is the most important part, because it distributes the weight of the load over the body. Frames are usually made of steel, aluminum, or magnesium. A few manufacturers also make hard plastic frames.

Steel frames are strong enough, but their weight is a disadvantage. Aluminum and magnesium frames are the lightest, with aluminum being the most popular and usually the least expensive. A good quality frame will cost $25-$40. When selecting a frame, one should be especially concerned about quality, because an inferior frame is a bad buy at any price.

When viewed from the side, the frame will have the shape of an elongated "S", and this should conform to the person's back. The quality of a frame is indicated by the kind of joints it has. If the joints are brazed, soldered, or bolted, the frame will not be as strong as if the joints were welded. Welded joints often have the appearance of being irregular and handmade, but welded joints are clearly the preferred kind.

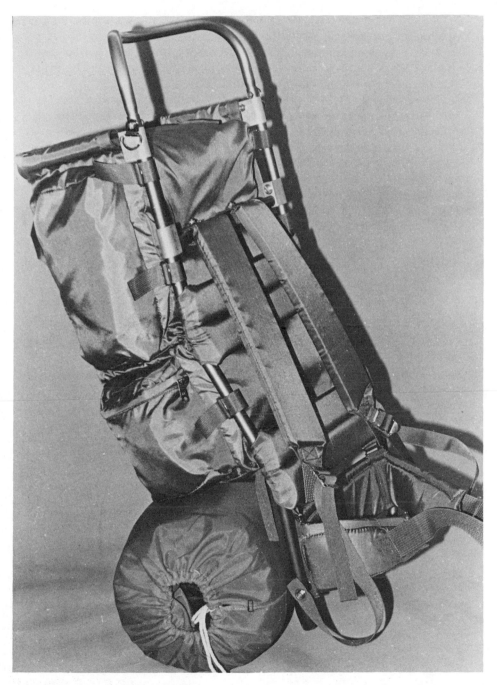

Figure 2-1. Full size pack with an aluminum frame. Notice the frame has *bolted* joints. The shoulder straps and waistband are well padded.

One can test the rigidity of a frame by putting the frame on the floor and bracing the bottom rails with the feet, then twisting the top with the hands, using a reasonable amount of force. Welded, soldered, and brazen joints will not allow much give. Bolted joints will allow more give. The frame should return to its original shape with no detrimental effects.

Check for any cracks in the joints and reject any frame which has even the slightest crack. The reputation of the manufacturer combined with the price tag are also important considerations.

The frame will have back panels which wrap around the it so that the loaded pack rests against the person's back. The panels should be adjustable so as to provide a custom fit. The lower band should rest on the upper slope of the buttocks. The upper panel should fit across the shoulder blades. Some frames have one large back panel made of nylon mesh. This enhances breathability and reduces sweating along the back underneath the panel.

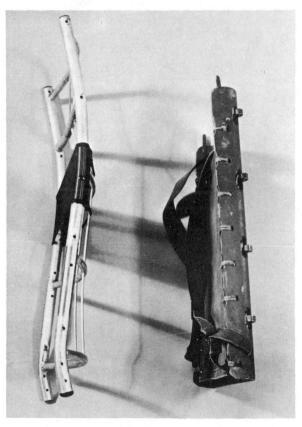

Figure 2-2. A typical modern pack frame (left) as contrasted with a military type frame (right). This modern frame is made of aluminum with *welded* joints.

Figure 2-3. Back panel which holds the pack away from the body and provides for adequate ventilation.

Shoulder Straps and Waist Belts

The **shoulder straps** should be wide and well padded where they come in contact with the shoulders, and narrow under the armpits. They must also be adjustable and should be easily released. When wearing the backpack, the straps should ride close to the neck rather than too far out on the shoulders.

A substantial and comfortable **waist belt** that is properly adjusted is one of the most important features of a pack frame. It helps hold the load close to the body, and takes a good part (50 percent or more) of the load off the shoulders. On some pack frames the waist belt is a full belt with the frame attaching into the back portion of the belt, while in other cases the waist belt is two half-belts attached to the lower portion of the two side pieces of the frame. Most experienced backpackers prefer a full belt. A two-piece belt tends to hold the frame tight to the back, while a full belt allows some "floating" of the pack as you walk. Full waist belts are available as a separate accessory at about $10 each. They are usually about four inches in width and padded generously.

The Pack Bag

The bag obviously must correspond to the frame in size so that it will fit the frame at the points of attachment. The three-quarter length bag is the most popular because of its versatility, and it is less expensive than a full length bag. Unless there is a reason to do otherwise, you ought to buy the specific bag that was made to fit the frame in order to avoid a less than perfect fit.

Certainly the material from which the bag is made and the construction at the seams and zippers are prime considerations. The bag will need to withstand considerable stress and rough handling. If it is not substantially constructed, it simply will not hold up. Some bags are made of water repellent material, but **waterproof** nylon is much preferred, especially in rainy climates. Breathability of the fabric is not as important in pack bags as it is in tents and clothing. The waterproof coating (urethane) should be on the inside of the bag because the outside is subject to scuffing. The sewing at the seams should be done with at least medium size synthetic thread. Synthetic thread is stronger than cotton thread; however, cotton coated dacron is acceptable. Reinforced stitching should be used at the ends of all seams and at points of stress. The seams should be coated with seam sealer.

Some bags consist of only one large compartment with small side pockets. But most three-quarter size or full-size bags have two major compartments, one upper and one lower, with two or more side pockets. These compartments make for easy access to items in the pack. The side pockets are very handy for camp accessories such as pocket knife, water container, first aid kit, matches, and other items that you might want to use along the trail. The pockets should have button flaps or zippers and the zippers should be highly durable. A narrow cloth flap that hangs over the zipper and completely covers it is important in order to protect the zipper from water and dirt. Zippers should be kept free of loose threads or other material that could catch and damage them.

The top flap of the main compartment should be large enough to cover generously the complete top of the pack, and it must fit around the edges in such a way as to keep rain and snow out of the compartment. The flap should be fastened with tie strings, thus affording flexibility as to how the flap fits over the load.

Possibly the most important feature of the pack is its durability at the points of attachment to the frame. If it becomes worn or torn at the attachment, it becomes useless.

Internal Framed Packs

Packs with frames built into the interior of the packs have gained in popularity during recent years. The internal framed pack has the advantage of combining the pack and frame into a single unit, and it has more shape

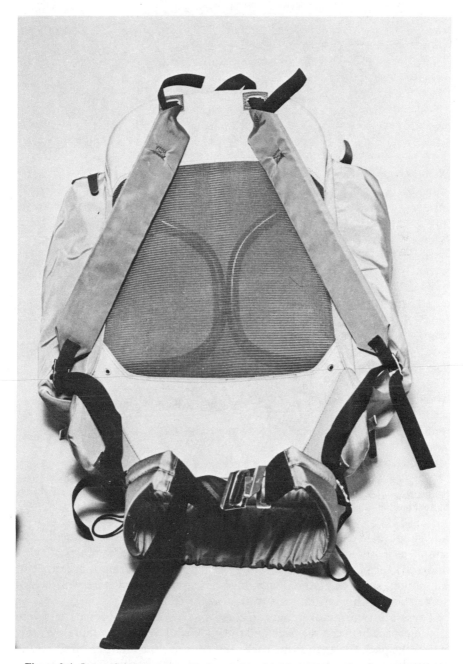

Figure 2-4. Internal frame pack with detachable shoulder straps and waist belt. Notice a portion of internal frame visible through the back panel.

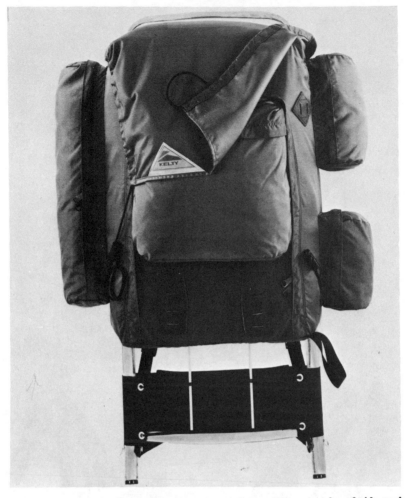

Figure 2-5. Top flap partially secured in place and two different styles of side pockets. Notice flaps over zippers and leather panels toward bottom to aid in strapping gear to the bottom portion of the pack frame.

and support than the rucksack. The frames of these packs are sometimes as simple as a stiff pad and sometimes relatively complex assemblies of tubes and rods forming X, H, U, or ladder structures. The frames are made of aluminum, steel, or plastic. Some internal framed packs have a waistbelt of some sort which transfers part of the weight to the hips.

There are two disadvantages to these packs: (a) they provide less ventilating space between the pack and the back which results in more sweating where the pack fits against the back; and (b) since the internal frame has no adjustable features, finding a pack that fits satisfactorily is sometimes difficult.

Frameless Packs

Developed only recently, this kind of pack is now manufactured by several companies, and it has gained rapidly in popularity. The concept of the pack is that it lets the spine, back portion of the rib cage, and hips of the packer substitute for the pack frame. It is imperative that this kind of pack be loaded correctly so that the pack fits the contour of the back and hips. If this is done, a portion of the weight is effectively transferred to the hips and the pack fits comfortably all the way up the back. A pack without a frame gives a person greater freedom of movement and the total weight of the pack is reduced by the amount the frame would weigh. Futhermore, you never have to worry about a broken frame. The obvious disadvantage is the relative lack of ventilation between the pack and the person's back.

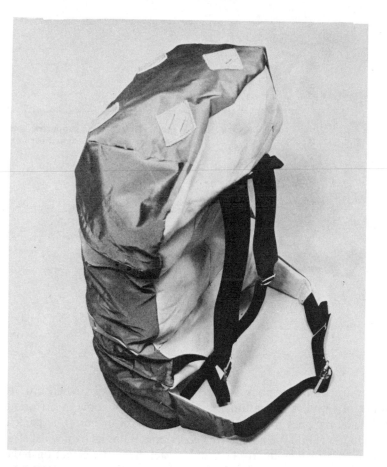

Figure 2-6. Frameless pack designed both for light use and to fit the contour of the middle and upperback.

Rucksacks

The rucksack is a small pack that is usually supported entirely by the shoulders, and it rides relatively low on the back. Rucksacks have the advantage of keeping the center of gravity low, and this makes them easier to handle over rough terrain or while climbing rocks and cliffs where balance is of great importance. Rucksacks also are less bulky and are well suited for a one-day or overnight hike. Because rucksacks, whether framed or unframed, are hung on the shoulders, they are uncomfortable on long trips when heavily loaded. But they are quite desirable for light loads and short trips.

Figure 2-7. Rucksack supported totally with the shoulder straps—designed for light use.

Waist Packs

The waist or fanny pack is useful for one-day trips when only a small amount of supplies and a lunch are needed. They come in different sizes, with the larger ones measuring about 6 x 6 x 18 inches. The pack is contoured to fit around the back of the waist, and it has its own waist strap with a buckle that fastens in front. A waist pack has little effect on balance or mobility, and it can be used effectively to carry items that you want to get to easily, such as camera equipment, snacks, etc.

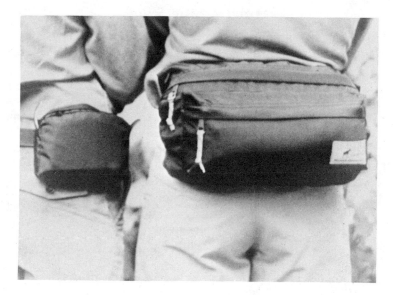

Figure 2-8. Waist pack and belt pack. (Photo by Geoffry Johnson)

Loading the Pack

The experienced backpacker will arrange the items in his pack essentially the same every time. There are two basic rules to follow: (1) place heavy items relatively high and close to the back; and (2) place items that you need to get to first in accessible locations.

Weight distribution is of utmost importance. The advantage of packing the heavier items close to the body and relatively high is that it keeps the weight close to the body's line of gravity. In fact, the weight can be placed over the body's center of gravity by leaning the trunk slightly forward which is the natural body stance when carrying a loaded pack. This means that the lower compartment and the part farthest away from the body should be filled with the lighter items. Items which need to be readily accessible should be placed near the openings of the pack, in the exterior pockets, or in pockets of one's clothing.

If a three quarter length bag is used, the sleeping gear should be lashed to the lower part of the frame, while in the case of a full length packbag, the sleeping gear is placed in the bottom. If the sleeping bag is outside the packbag, it is a good idea to enclose it in a nylon or plastic bag. Wet sleeping gear from a sudden rainstorm can result in a very uncomfortable night.

Hoisting the Pack

Hoisting a heavy pack onto your back can be a little bit of a challenge but certainly not a difficult problem. Here are some useful methods to keep in mind:

1. Use the buddy method where your companion rests your pack high on his thigh with the shoulder straps facing you. Get your body low enough to place your arms through the shoulder straps, then assist your companion as he lifts your pack into place. In turn you can do the same for him.

2. Place your pack in an upright position on a rock, stump, or embankment at a height which will allow you to turn your back into position and thread your arms through the shoulder straps.

3. Lift your pack to the proper height and press it against a tree or ledge while you turn your hips underneath it and support it in that position while you harness yourself into the shoulder straps and waistbelt.

4. Lift the pack high onto your right thigh with the frame facing you. Then dip the right shoulder into the straps and swing the pack around on the right shoulder blade while supporting the weight of the pack with the right hand grasping the right bottom of the pack frame. Thread the left arm into the shoulder strap and bounce the pack into proper position.

Figure 2-9. One method of hoisting a loaded pack.

Care and Maintenance

Avoid packing bottles filled with any kind of substance for a bottle might break inside the pack. Avoid packing objects with sharp corners or edges where they might do damage to the fabric. Do not drop the pack when taking it off because the impact of a heavy load can damage both the frame and the seams as well as items inside the pack. At night, hang the pack on a tree or place it next to you to protect it from animals which might chew or scratch on it or drag it away.

Between trips, care of the pack is rather simple. Hose the pack off both inside and out and let it dry thoroughly before putting it away. Store it in a dry, relatively cool place free of dust and dirt and protection from rodents.

Relative to maintenance, the old cliche, "a stitch in time saves nine" is certainly applicable. After returning from each trip examine your pack thoroughly for damage and make the needed repairs at that time so you don't forget before the next trip. It's advisable to store your backpacking items in your pack except a sleeping bag which ought to be flocked. This increases the chance that you will know where to find the items when you prepare for the next trip.

A minimum repair kit ought to be taken on every trip. The most useful item to include is a supply of light nylon cord. With this, you can splint a broken frame, lace together a tear, and repair other forms of damage. Adhesive tape and ripstop nylon with adhesive backing are other useful items. These can also be used in splinting a frame, but they are especially useful in repairing tears in a pack. In order to obtain the best results, the repair tape should be applied on the inside or both sides. In connection with maintenance and repairs, the most useful concept is "prevention is better than cure."

3
Appropriate Footwear and Clothing

The fact that we live in a world that moves crisis by crisis, causes contact with nature to take on even greater significance.

Walking is truly the name of the game for the backpacker. For this reason, proper care of the feet is of paramount importance. Purchasing poorly constructed or ill fitting footwear is false economy, and it can result in agonizing experiences and disappointment. A backpacker with blisters or aching feet will travel neither far nor happily. Furthermore, one who gets too hot or too cold or suffers the discomforts of ill-fitted clothing will have less than a satisfying experience.

Hiking Boots

Some hikers prefer boots of heavy and solid construction. However, many prefer a medium weight boot which is fairly substantial and easy to handle. For short trips on easy terrain, some hikers prefer low cut hiking shoes or well constructed athletic shoes.

Figure 3-1. Three weights of hiking boots: light (top), medium (center) and heavy (bottom)—all of similar style and with vibram tread.

The more important characteristics of footwear are comfort, support, durability and weight. Here are some specific features to watch for when selecting boots:

● The better boots will have several layers of leather laminated together and then sewn as well as glued to a Vibran sole. Usually, lesser quality boots will have only a thin layer of leather to which the Vibran is attached, and the sole will be only glued and not stitched. Some of the very best boots also have screws driven upward through the heel and the instep to support further the glue and stitching.

● The U.S. Army Research Institute of Environmental Medicine claims that carrying one pound on the foot demands the same amount of energy as carrying six pounds on the back. So weight of the footwear is obviously important in terms of fatigue.

● It is desirable that the upper section of the boot be composed of full grain cowhide, preferably one piece with no seams except up the back. Split cowhide is acceptable but it is less durable and it stretches more. The tongue underneath the lacing should be padded and extend well above the top of the laces.

● Many of the better boots have a ski flap which crosses over on top of the tongue at the upper portion of the boot. This helps keep out moisture and foreign objects.

● In terms of lacing, the lesser quality boots usually have eyelets placed in the leather, whereas the better boots have D-rings which are riveted to the leather, and some of them have speed hooks for the upper portion of the lacing. Woven nylon laces are preferred over leather because leather laces stretch and rot.

Figure 3-2. Vibran tread on the sole of a boot.

● It is especially important to have no metal parts or rough surfaces protruding on the interior of the boot. The scree which circles the opening of the boot should be covered with soft leather over a thin section of foam rubber.

● The shape of the boot should help anchor the foot to the sole. A well designed boot, when laced, will allow very little movement of the heel. A hard toe cap is desirable in rough and rocky terrain.

Remember, the more important characteristics are comfort, support, durability and relative light weight. Well-constructed boots having most of the characteristics explained above range in price from $40-$80.

Proper Fit

Boots purchased at bargain counters are poor deals if they do not fit properly. Always try on both boots—many people have one foot which is slightly larger than the other. The boot should be large enough so that the toes do not touch the end. When the boot is unlaced and the foot slid all the way forward, there should be enough room to place the index finger between the heel and the back of the boot. The boot should be wide enough to be comfortable but not loose. The area of the lacing should be spread far enough to allow further tightening after the boot is broken in. Most boots will stretch slightly in width but not in length.

It's a good idea to shop for boots in the afternoon or evening because the

Figure 3-3. Three different styles of hiking boots: regular ankle height with split leather exterior (left), high top with smooth leather exterior (center), and high top with rubberized foot portion for marshy terrain (right).

feet tend to swell slightly from blood accumulation after spending part of the day in the erect position. Always wear two pair of socks when trying on boots, the same as you wear on backpack trips. Two pair provides better cushion for the feet, absorbs the moisture better, and allows a small amount of slippage between the socks, thus reducing the possibility of wearing blisters on the feet.

Part of achieving a near perfect fit is to break in the boots properly. The best method is to simply wear the boots during daily activities or on short hikes until they are thoroughly broken in. Always wear the same kind of socks during the breaking in period as will be worn during backpacking. Do not break in boots by filling them with water as some people recommend, because this contributes to destruction of both the material and the construction.

A near perfect fit should result if you work with a good salesperson, buy a good product, exercise thorough attention and good judgment, and follow the described procedure for breaking in new boots.

> **ONE OR TWO THIN INNER SOCKS PLUS A HEAVY WOOL SOCK WILL MINIMIZE FOOT BLISTERS. PUT ON CLEAN INNER SOCKS DAILY.**

Care of Hiking Boots

Good quality boots are very durable and can take about everything you give them on the trail, but there are a few things that can contribute to their destruction. Heat is the most common culprit for ruining boots. If leather boots are force dried in front of a fire, the leather tends to shrink and crack. Toe warming at the fire causes some of this effect, and storing boots too close to a furnace or heater can also cause damage.

You can splash through mud on the trail all you please, but at the end of the day boots need to be cleansed. As mud dries, it pulls the natural oils out of the leather and this causes hardening and cracking. It also damages the cement used in holding the boot together.

If boots are to remain water repellent, they require waterproof treatment from time to time. The first treatment should be done when the boots are new. Oil tanned boots should be treated with an oil or grease compound, whereas chrome tanned boots require treatment with wax or silicone. The salesperson should be able to advise you on the proper kind of waterproofing for the particular boots.

Figure 3-4. Complete boot care kit: waterproofer, leather conditioner to prevent rot, and stitch lock. (Photo used by permission of the Early Winter Co.)

WET BOOTS SHOULD BE PLACED ON A STAKE UPSIDE DOWN TO BE DRIED AND AIRED, AWAY FROM FIRE AND HOT, DIRECT SUN.

Clothing

Clothing can make a big difference in your ability to remain comfortable and adequately protected from the elements. Since clothing is a personal matter, no one can establish set rules that are equally applicable to everybody. But there are some important guidelines among which are that clothing should be durable, relatively light, and warm for its weight. The layer system of clothing is best, and it is just what it sounds like. You add or remove layers as the temperature varies.

Keep in mind that, when you're involved in muscular activity, your body generates more heat and, when you become stationary, the rate of heat production reduces. For this reason, when you stop hiking, it is sometimes advisable to add a layer of clothing so you don't chill. (For more information about this, refer to the chapter on hypothermia and hyperthermia.)

Underclothing

When backpacking during mild weather, there should be little, if any, change in your underclothing from that which you normally wear. Many people prefer underwear made of cotton because it is soft and comfortable against the skin and it absorbs perspiration readily. It does not cause a clammy feeling as some of the synthetic fabrics do. Some hikers prefer fine wool, because it retains high insulating value even when damp. Thermal underwear of various styles is available, and should be considered whenever you anticipate temperatures of near freezing and below.

Fishnet underwear has certain advantages. In warm weather when the outer shirt is loosened at the neck, sleeves and waist, the fishnet fabric allows free circulation of air underneath. This enhances ventilation and helps in cooling the body. When the weather gets colder, the outer layers can be tightened at the neck, wrists and waist, and the fishnet fabric then creates dead air pockets close to the skin which hold in body heat, thus having a thermal effect. To provide maximum warmth, the underwear should reach over the ankles and wrists and fit snugly at those points. The disadvantage of the fishnet fabric is that it is less comfortable against the skin than smooth cotton.

Shirts, Sweaters and Jackets

If an undershirt is not worn, then the outer shirt should be made of cotton; a cotton flannel is preferred. A plaid color is desirable because it will not show dirt readily. If a cotton or fishnet undershirt is worn, then either a cotton flannel or light wool outer shirt is satisfactory. Wool is a hardy material which is considerably warmer than cotton for the same weight, and its insulating characteristic is retained much better when damp than other fabrics. The outer shirt should have long sleeves which can be rolled up or down, depending on the outside temperature and the need for protection of the arms from the sun and insects. Pockets with button-top flaps are useful features.

A good sweater or jacket should always be taken on a backpacking trip because the nights and mornings are often quite cool, even in midsummer. Instead of taking a heavy parka, it is preferable to have several lighter layers which can be added and taken off as needed. A good combination is a wool sweater along with a light outer jacket which is windproof and water repellent. If cold temperatures are expected, you ought to carry an extra sweater or a warm vest or parka. It is important to keep these items of clothing dry as possible so they will not lose their insulating effect. Button-flap or zipper pockets are desirable in the jacket.

A relatively new product known as **Gore-Tex** is now in use by several manufacturers of outdoor clothing. This amazing material is breathable while at the same time it is waterproof and windproof. Gore-Tex is a form of resin which is spread into a very thin sheet (.001 of an inch) and sandwiched between layers of nylon or other tough fabric. Every square inch of it has nine million pores. Each pore is large enough to allow water vapor to pass through, but too small for water in liquid form to penetrate. Hence, body vapor can escape, but raindrops cannot get through. It seems likely that in the future this material will be used extensively in outdoor clothing. In fact it is already becoming very popular.

Figure 3-5. Some prefer the versatility afforded by a long sleeve shirt and a sleeveless vest. In addition, a lightweight outer jacket is especially useful when made of material that is wind resistant, water repellant and breathable.

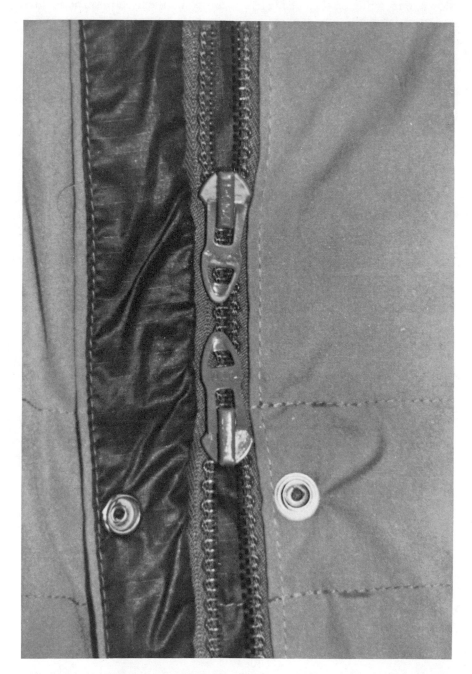

Figure 3-6. In clothing items, consider the value of a sturdy two-way zipper, and a button overflap.

Trousers

Almost any kind of trousers that fit properly are suitable if they are in good repair, made of tough material, and suitable for the particular climate. It is important for trousers to be quite loose through the crotch and around the upper leg to allow freedom of movement. Be sure that the seams are in good condition and the fabric is not worn thin or otherwise in poor repair. The trousers should be long enough to cover the ankles, but keep in mind that trousers which are too long or too full around the ankles present a snagging problem in heavy underbrush. An adequate number of substantial pockets is more than a useful convenience. The trousers should be made of a tough fabric that will endure hard use, yet one that is comfortable to wear. A fabric that has a high degree of water repellency has an advantage because of the presence of morning dew and the possibility of rain showers. For use in wet and cool climates, Gore-Tex trousers, leggers or gaiters are available.

Shorts are worn by some backpackers in warm weather. If you choose to wear shorts, never go on a very long hike without a pair of long trousers in case they are needed for protection from the sun, insects or cold.

Figure 3-7. Gore-Tex gaiters—waterproof, windproof and breathable. (Photo used by permission of the Early Winter Co.)

Socks, Hats and Gloves

Socks are a very important part of your clothing. The type and number of socks worn is much a matter of personal choice. Some prefer only one pair of heavy cotton socks, while others prefer wool socks. Most people involved in vigorous sports or long distance hiking wear two pair of socks—usually a thinner pair next to the foot and a thicker pair over the top. This arrangement allows some slippage between the socks and thereby reduces friction between the shoe and the foot, thus minimizing the chance of developing blisters. Whatever your preference in socks, keep in mind that protection against blisters is of utmost importance, and the socks you wear are one of the keys to the prevention of this problem. A duplicate set of socks should always be taken along if you're hiking for more than a day. Some people even choose to change socks during a long day's hike. It's a good idea to wash the soiled socks at the end of each day and let them dry overnight. This will provide a clean pair of socks in your pack each morning. When backpacking in cold weather, it is wise to carry a third pair of socks to be used for sleeping. Never wear to bed those socks which you have worn all day on the trail because they will be soiled and moist.

A hat is not absolutely essential, but it can add a great deal of comfort in certain weather conditions. The head receives a large portion of the body's blood supply; thus, it is very critical in temperature regulation. The old saying, "If your feet get cold, put on a hat," possesses a good deal of truth. More heat can be lost through the head than any other comparable surface area of the body.

Conversely, if there is a scorching sun beating down on you, a hat can protect the head from overheating and help prevent discomfort and possibly heat stroke. Also, a hat with a shade will keep the sun off the face, ears, and back of the neck, thus protecting these areas from sunburn. If the hat is good for sun protection, the chances are that it will also be an advantage in rainy conditions.

Climatic conditions will strongly influence the kind of hat preferred or whether one is needed at all. In some locations, protection against rain and cold is the principle purpose of the hat, whereas in other cases, protection against the sun or insects is the main purpose. A stocking-type cap is useful for a variety of reasons, including its use as a temperature control while sleeping in cool weather.

Gloves are not used by many backpackers unless the weather is cold. But it is true that a light pair of cotton gloves or thin leather gloves is useful around camp for chopping wood, handling hot pans, and protecting the hands against cold in the evening and early morning. Gloves are definitely an optional item, and whether they are included in the pack depends on the weather conditions and personal preference.

Figure 3-8. A french jungle hat is suitable for both dry and wet climates. A head net, with an aluminum rim to hold it away from the face, is valuable in insect-infested areas.

Rain Gear

Manufacturers of rain clothing face one of the same challenges as the manufacturers of tents—the need for material which is both waterproof and breathable. The material known as Gore-Tex, described earlier, fits the need rather well, and it is now being used by several companies in the making of rain gear. Tent manufacturers have solved their problem through double layering (roof plus rainfly), but this is impractical for rain clothing.

The most popular type of rain clothing is the poncho, which is usually nothing more than a large piece of plastic or nylon with a hole in the center for the head and sometimes a hood attached. It is important that the poncho be large enough to fit over both the person and the pack. Ponchos fit loosely and are therefore hard to control in windy weather. They also snag easily on branches. A poncho is versatile in the sense that, if you don't have a shelter, it can be used to cover your sleeping bag or your supplies in the case of rain. Also the poncho makes a good ground cloth on which to lay the sleeping bag.

There are other kinds of rain gear to consider, such as lightweight waterproof pants and a slicker or raincoat, and a rain hat. Rubberized rain gear is quite heavy and bulky and this makes it quite impractical for backpacking, although in wet climates some backpackers do use it. Occasionally, you will see a backpacker who carries a fold-up umbrella. Actually this is a fairly practical idea, but for many it seems too domestic.

If you choose not to carry rain gear but still want some protection, a reasonably good raincoat can be improvised with the use of a large plastic trash bag. Simply cut holes in the sides near the two corners through which the arms can fit (see Figure **3-11**). A smaller plastic bag can be used as an improvised rain hat. Plastic bags are easy to carry and they can often be used for multiple purposes.

In wet weather it is especially important that your hiking boots are in good repair and thoroughly treated with the proper kind of waterproofing material.

Figure 3-9. Improvised raincoat and hat cover made of plastic bags.

4
Selecting the Right Sleeping Gear

People must also have a sanctuary of unspoiled land—a place of solitude where they may turn their thoughts inward and wonder at the miracles of creation.

The kind of sleeping equipment you have can make the difference between an enjoyable experience or a long, uncomfortable night. The features that separate a poor sleeping bag from a truly good one have to do with design, workmanship, and filler material. So, in selecting a bag, give adequate attention to all of these factors. Even though overall comfort is important, the principal feature of a sleeping bag is the ability to keep you warm. The warmth rating that is needed in a particular bag to suit your purpose needs to be considered in light of the following:

- Each person's metabolism (ability to generate heat) is different, meaning that certain people sleep colder or warmer than others.

- The outside temperature will vary greatly depending on the season of the year and your geographic location. Also, whether you customarily sleep inside a tent or under the stars is a consideration.

- In a sleeping bag, your body weight compresses the portion on which you lie and compressed insulation loses much of its warmth. Therefore, if you use a foam pad or other type of insulating material underneath, the bag will be more effective.

39

Sleeping Bag Design

Some sleeping bags are rectangular in shape while others are tapered. A tapered bag is cut to fit the shape of the body—narrower at the feet and wider at the shoulders. Bags are often designed to fit snugly at the neck and some bags have a hood with a drawstring which leaves only the face exposed. The more extreme tapered bags are called mummy bags. The advantages of the different designs are as follows:

1. Rectangular bags are more comfortable because they have more space inside, but they are larger and therefore heavier; also they are less efficient because of more inside space to be warmed by the body and more surface area through which heat can escape. In addition, rectangular bags usually are not designed to fit snugly around the shoulders and neck and this contributes to their inefficiency.

2. A well designed mummy bag is the most efficient sleeping bag because it fits the contour of the body and wraps snugly around the shoulders and neck. Furthermore, many mummy bags have hoods which add even more to their warmth efficiency. By fitting the contour of the body, the mummy bag has a minimum amount of space inside to be heated and minimum surface area through which heat escapes. Mummy bags are made of less material and therefore are lighter and less bulky. The one disadvantage is lack of comfort due to the lack of inside space.

3. Moderately tapered bags represent a compromise which many people prefer because for them a mummy bag is too uncomfortable and a rectangular bag is too inefficient and bulky.

Filler Material

Sleeping bag warmth is directly related to the fact that heat escapes very slowly across dead air space. The thicker the air space, the slower heat loss. The two main factors which influence the desirability of a filler material are: (1) the thickness it provides per unit of weight (loft); and (2) its ability to spring back to its original thickness or loft after being compressed. Of the frequently used fillers, the one that provides these characteristics the best is **original down**. Down provides more thickness per weight than other fillers, and its ability to regain loft after being compressed remains at almost the 100 percent level for a long time.

It is often claimed that goose down is superior to duck down, but the most reliable information indicates that, when the quality is equal, the two kinds of down have about the same warmth factor. It is interesting to note that the very best down in the world comes from the Eider duck, due to its

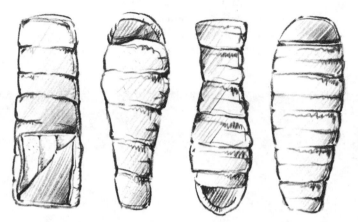

Figure 4-1. Illustrations of the various sleeping bag designs: rectangular (top), two styles of mummy bags (middle), and moderately tapered (bottom).

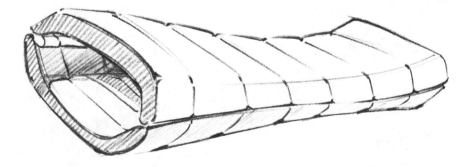

Figure 4-2. Illustration of the loft of a fully fluffed down-filled bag. Also shown are the baffle along the inside of the zipper (upper side) and the differential cut of the inside and outside walls. This cut enhances loft by reducing wall pressure.

incredible ability to loft. Unfortunately, Eider down is extremely expensive and not very prevalent.

Two pounds of high quality down in a well constructed bag will provide enough warmth for most backpacking experiences. Three pounds of high quality down is considered satisfactory for sub-freezing temperatures. For temperatures which approach 0°F, a three pound bag will need to be supplemented with more than a normal amount of warm night clothing, or a four pound down bag will be needed. Actually loft is a more reliable measure of warmth than poundage of filler. But, with high-quality bags, loft and poundage correspond closely.

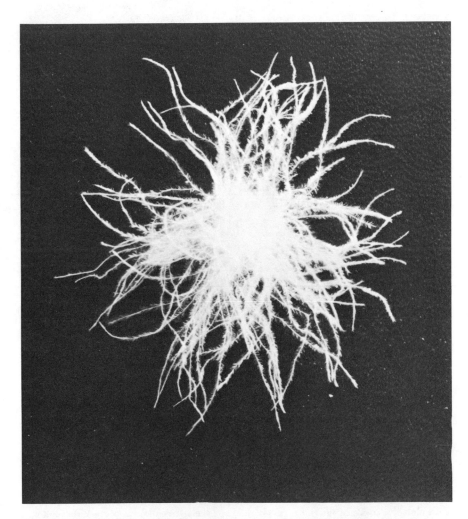

Figure 4-3. This fluffed fiber of down illustrates how fibers expand to fill space.

Original down is better than reprocessed down, which provides only about 80 percent as much warmth per unit of weight. Original down is expensive and in short supply. (A good quality sleeping bag containing 2-3 lbs. of original down will cost about $200). Therefore, reprocessed down is used by some manufacturers. When buying a down filled bag, it is important to know whether the down is original or reprocessed.

Down is a by-product of the food industry, with most of it coming from domestic geese and ducks in Asia. Some of it comes from Europe, and a small amount from the United States. The quality of much of the down received by equipment manufacturers is dubious for two reasons: (1) The most prevalent kind of down is from domestic waterfowl slaughtered at a young age before the down reaches maturity. This down has less warmth efficiency than mature down; and (2) Rather than pure down clusters, the down used by all manufacturers is a mixture of down, feathers, and foreign materials. There are advantages to having some feathers and fiber, but if the proportion gets too high, it drastically dilutes the effectiveness of the filler. The state of California has passed a law that down filler cannot be labeled as such unless it is composed of at least 70 percent down clusters, with no more than 30 percent feathers and other materials.

Another aspect of down quality that can be tested and controlled is **fill power**. Fill power refers to the volume filled by one ounce of filling material. Higher fill power means greater loft without adding weight or losing compressibility.

If you buy a down bag, it's important to learn as much as possible about the kind of down and its quality. Do not assume that all filler materials labeled "down" have the same quality or the same warmth efficiency.

In spite of its overall superiority, down does have certain disadvantages: (1) it loses practically all of its loft when wet; and (2) it takes a relatively long time to dry once it becomes wet (forty-eight hours of drying time is sometimes required for a completely soaked down bag.) Also, down is a poor insulator when compressed between the ground and body. For this reason, an insulating pad is needed.

Dacron Hollofil II or Polarguard are the best man-made fillers on the market. Compared to down, Hollofil and Polarguard provide 85-90 percent as much warmth per unit of weight because their loft is less. Bags filled with these polyester fibers dry much faster than down. In addition, a Hollofil or Polarguard bag insulates between the ground and body better than down, thus causing a sleeping pad to be less essential. Polarguard is made of long fibers whereas Hollofil is made of short fibers. Each manufacturer claims certain advantages related to this difference. But overall, these two synthetic products are approximately equal.

There are sleeping bags on the market now which combine the best of man-made filler and down. These bags have a bottom made of Hollofil or Polarguard and a top filled with down. This combination gives the sleeping bag the superior insulating quality between the body and ground afforded synthetic filler and the unequaled loft of down on the top. Polarguard insulates about as well as Hollofil II but doesn't drape around your body quite as well. In its favor, though, PolarGuard filaments don't shift around, so they require less fabric baffling. Well-made bags with either of these polyesters can be terrific.

There are other filler materials used in different quality sleeping bags. For instance, a product known as Hollofil 88 is frequently used in medium priced bags. Whatever kind of bag you buy, it is important to learn as much as you can about the characteristics of original down which is the measuring stick for all other fillers.

An interesting discovery has recently been made by the 3-M Company. It is a new fiber which they call **Thinsulate**. This fiber has undergone extensive testing and is just coming into use. According to the laboratory tests, Thinsulate has a higher warmth efficiency than down, with Thinsulate having a warmth rating of 1.8 as compared to 1.0 for down and .9 for the best polyester. The preliminary reports indicate that Thinsulate has most of the advantages of polyester fibers while producing more warmth than down. Obviously, more experimentation and practical use will be needed before the preliminary claims can be confirmed, but if the reports are anywhere near correct, you can look for Thinsulate to become very popular in sleeping bags and cold weather clothing.

Internal Construction

The internal construction of a sleeping bag influences the uniform thickness of the filler and the ability of the filler to expand completely. High quality internal construction can cause the bag to be adequate at several degrees colder than if the construction is poor. The primary function of internal construction is to hold the filler in position so that it does not become bunched up, thus leaving some areas with little or no filler. The filler should not be compressed as a result of the construction, but rather the construction should enhance the ability of the filler to expand. Durability of the internal baffles is very important.

There are five basic kinds of internal construction, and some manufacturers use slight variations of these basic construction types.

A **simple quilted** construction, which is the least desirable, is used in some inexpensive bags. With this kind of construction the insulation is spread unevenly and there is practically no insulation along the sewing lines.

The **laminated** type of construction is essentially two simple quilted layers sewn together with the thick and thin areas alternated. This design is much better for warmth than the simple quilted construction, but it uses a lot of fabric on the interior, and this adds to the weight of the bag.

Many outdoorsmen feel that **box quilted** construction is the very best.

This results in compartments three to four inches wide formed by partitions connected to the outer and inner shells. This kind of construction causes almost total uniformity of thickness, and it adds a minimum amount of weight.

Two other effective kinds of interior construction which are used in some of the better bags are the slant tube and overlapping tube. There construction types are effective in holding the filler in place and providing uniform thickness. The disadvantage of these bags is that they have a little more fabric on the interior then box quilted bags, adding slightly to the weight.

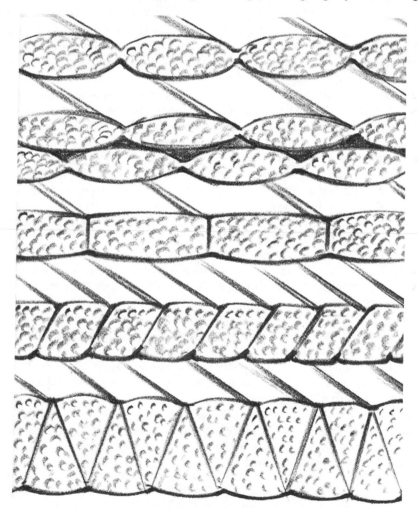

Figure 4-4. Five kinds of internal construction (in order from top to bottom): simple quilted, laminated or double quilted, box quilted, slant tube, and overlapping tube.

External Construction

It is important for the outer and inner shells of the bag to be made of fabric which is very strong, highly durable, breathable, wind resistant, water repellent, and easy to clean. Ripstop nylon and taffeta are the materials most frequently used for shell construction in top quality bags. The shell should be of a tight weave so that none of the filler can escape through the fabric pores. The new material known as Gore-Tex, which is both breathable and waterproof, is being used by some manufacturers. The basic characteristics of this material were described in the previous chapter in the section titled **Shirts, Sweaters and Jackets**. Also, it is now possible to purchase a Gore-Tex outer cover which is slightly larger than a sleeping bag in a rolled out position with a flap that extends over the head region. These breathable, waterproof Gore-Tex shells are designed to substitute for tents for the backpacker who wants to travel light.

Most bags have a zipper; however, a few fit over the body like a sock and have no zipper. In some cases the zipper might be three-quarters of the bag's length or full length plus the width across the bottom. A shorter length zipper has an advantage in cold weather because there will be less heat loss along the zipper. The zipper should be of top quality so it does not malfunction or become broken. A substantial high quality nylon zipper is preferred over a metal zipper, because a nylon zipper results in less heat loss and is less likely to become clogged. There should be a baffle on the inside of the zipper (filled with the same material as the bag) which presses against the zipper to reduce heat loss. This is a very important feature. Some bags have a double zipper with a baffle between the two zippers.

A socklike bag with no zipper is quite acceptable if the construction around the shoulders and neck enables a snug fit for minimum heat loss. However, these bags are awkward to get in and out of in tight shelters. If the bag is to be used in a variety of temperatures during different seasons, a zipper has an advantage because you can adjust the warmth by sleeping with the zipper closed or partially open.

A well-constructed mummy bag will have additional room at the foot end in the form of a boxlike construction. This provides comfortable space for the feet, preventing them from pressing against the bag and thus reducing its thickness, and also preventing the wearing of a hole in the inner shell.

The fit of the bag, especially around the shoulders, neck, and head in the fully zipped position, is of prime importance, because a good amount of heat can be lost from this area if the bag is improperly designed.

Summary of Desirable Features of a Bag

● The outside shell, especially the bottom portion, should be made of ripstop nylon. The inside fabric should be tough but relatively soft and pleasant to the touch.

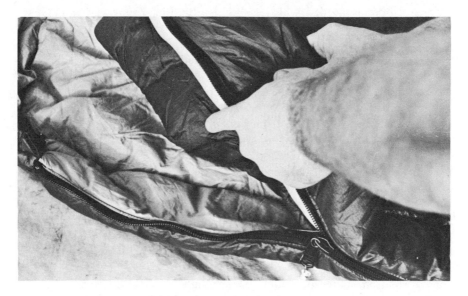

Figure 4-5. Heavy duty nylon zipper with down filled baffle behind it to prevent warm air from escaping.

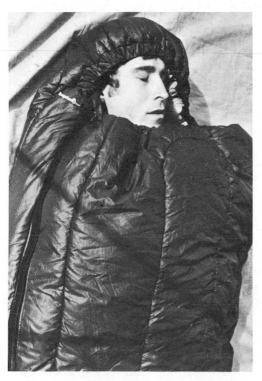

Figure 4-6. Some bags are designed to fit snugly around the shoulders, neck and head to prevent loss of heat.

● A zipper is needed which is highly durable, freeze resistant, snag resistant, and unzips from both top to bottom. A self-repairing nylon zipper is recommended.

● The draft flap, which is the insulated pad along the inside of the zipper, must be efficient in order to reduce the amount of heat loss. Some bags have a double flap and a few have two zippers with the flap between. It's an advantage to have the flap covered with webbing or other tough material along the zipper to protect it from becoming snagged.

● The thread used for sewing seams must be strong and durable. Cotton wrapped dacron or nylon is recommended.

● The baffling should be made of stretch material to reduce the chance of damage due to pressure on the walls.

● The particular style and dimension of the baffles is very important, and the most desirable style varies with the different kinds of filler. The important thing is that the baffles remain effective over the life expectancy of the bag in holding the filler in position so that the loft of the bag remains uniform.

● Insulation material, which has a high warmth efficiency for its weight, is of utmost importance. High quality down is still the most effective, proven product. However, Polyguard and Hollofil II are close seconds, and a new product called Thinsulate might prove better than down.

● A differential cut is important. This means that the inside shell is cut smaller than the outside shell so that the two shells are separated by the amount of the loft. This contributes to the bag's warmth efficiency.

● A hood and a collar with drawstrings might be desirable, depending upon the use the bag will receive and one's preference.

● The foot section should be flared or enlarged to make adequate room for the feet. Otherwise, pressure applied by the feet will reduce the loft.

● The **stuff bag** should be made of tough, waterproof material with a water protective top. The **storage bag** should be made of breathable fabric and be large enough to permit the bag to partially loft.

● Proper fit is essential. From the standpoint of **warmth,** the bag should be cut to fit the contours of the body in order to minimize the inside space. From the **comfort** point of view, the bag needs to be sufficiently roomy.

Ground Pad

A sleeping bag compresses with body weight, and this reduces the thickness and insulation underneath. Without adequate insulation between you and the ground, conduction occurs, causing you to lose body heat. An adequate ground pad is the best solution to this problem.

The days of making a mattress of pine boughs or other natural materials

Figure 4-7. This winter backpacker has a sleeping bag in the top of the pack and a foam pad attached at the bottom.

are gone because of ecological considerations. Besides, a foam pad or air mattress is better.

Lightweight, plastic **air mattresses** were popular until a few years ago. But they have gone by the wayside among most outdoorsmen because they puncture too easily. Thousands of inferior mattresses have been left in trailside garbage cans by disgruntled backpackers who thought they were prepared for a good night's rest.

The only kind of air mattress that ought to be considered is a good quality, medium-weight, nylon coated mattress. It will weigh about 2½ pounds and cost $15 to $25. A three-quarter length (hip length) is recommended in order to conserve on the amount of weight in your pack. Your lower legs and feet can get along without a mattress provided the area on which they lie is built up to the level of the mattress and there is adequate insulation underneath.

An air mattress should not be completely filled or it will lack comfort. Place the valve near your head so you can release or add air conveniently. (You will need to roll off the mattress to add air.) It is a good idea to open the valve as soon as you wake up in the morning so the weight of your body will cause the mattress to empty. This saves waiting time. It is advisable to place the mattress on a waterproof groundcloth (a sheet of plastic will do) to add insulation underneath and protect the mattress from becoming wet or punctured. A compact patch kit should always be carried with an air mattress.

Most backpackers today prefer a **foam pad** instead of an air mattress. A pad is lighter than a mattress but more bulky. A foam pad provides more insulation underneath, it's more convenient once you arrive at the campsite, and more reliable. The minimum dimensions you should consider are two feet wide and three-quarter length (hip length). Two inches would be maximum thickness; however, most backpackers prefer a thickness between three-fourths of an inch and an inch and a half. An inch and a half pad, 48 inches long, will compress into a rolled up bundle about 8 inches in diameter; whereas a 3/4 inch pad will roll to a bundle about 5 inches in diameter.

Among the foam pads there are open cell (polyurethane) and closed cell (ensolite) pads. It is not necessary for a closed cell pad to be covered with a waterproof nylon shell because its surface is water repellent. However, the pad will serve better and wear longer if it is covered. An open celled pad absorbs water very readily, like a sponge; therefore, it must be encased in a cover with a waterproof bottom. The best kind of cover is one made of waterproof nylon taffeta on the bottom and a cotton fabric on the top. Cotton offers better grip for a nylon sleeping bag and also breathes, allowing moisture to evaporate. It's important to have a zipper or flap in one end so the cover can be removed for cleaning. Obviously, the cotton side must be protected from rain or snow in order to keep the pad dry. If a pillow is desired, consider the use of a heavy self-sealing 12″ x 24″ plastic bag filled partially with air and wrapped in your sweater or towel. During the day it can be used for other purposes as needed.

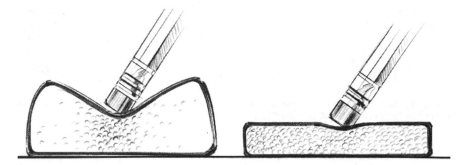

Figure 4-8. Two types of foam pads: soft open cell (left), and hard closed cell (right).

Care and Cleaning of Sleeping Bags

With proper care, a good sleeping bag can last for years, but poor care will rapidly diminish the bag's life expectancy. The outer shell of the sleeping bag is strong, but very thin. This thin shell must be protected from wear and snagging, especially if the bag is down filled. One should always take care to have a protective layer such as a pad or mattress, a sheet of plastic or the floor of the tent between the bottom of the bag and the ground. The nylon shell must be closely guarded against open flames and sparks, because a single spark can quickly melt a hole in the fabric. For this reason, avoid drying a sleeping bag close to the fire.

The inside shell of a sleeping bag also needs protection. The main problem here is with dirt and body oils. Some hikers use liners of nylon or cotton which can be removed and laundered. The liner keeps the inside of the bag clean, but it has the tendency to become displaced and may detract from the comfort of the bag. An alternative is to wear pajamas or long underwear and clean socks to bed. Keeping the body clean is also a very good practice. Consider wearing a stocking cap of some sort to cover the head. Unless it is raining, the sleeping bag should be turned inside out or opened up and aired for 20-30 minutes each morning to let collected moisture escape. Then fluff it thoroughly in preparation for the next use.

Between trips sleeping bags should not be stored in their stuff bags. The more time the bag spends in a tightly compressed condition, the greater the chance that it will lose loft. The bag should be hung, draped over a line, loosely rolled, or loosely stuffed in a large bag.

Figure 4-9. A nylon cover can help protect a foam pad from dirt, dampness and wear. This cover can be easily removed for cleaning.

Bags which are filled with polyester filler can be safely washed in warm water with a mild soap either by hand or in a front loading (tumble) washer adjusted to a delicate setting.

When cleaning down sleeping bags, one must be very careful. The cleaning of a down bag should be done infrequently—once a year if the bag is used often. The more times a down bag is cleaned, the greater the chance of losing loft.

One method is to take the bag to a reputable dry cleaner who has had successful experience cleaning down bags. After the bag has been cleaned, you must air it for three to four days until the solvent odor is gone. Some solvents have a destructive effect on down, so it is important that the cleaner know his business in this regard.

The best method of cleaning a down bag is to launder it by hand. This must be done with the utmost care. Following are instructions for hand washing a down bag:

Place the bag in a bathtub or other large container of warm (never hot) water containing very mild soap (not detergent). Press the bag into the soapy water starting at one end and keeping the other end dry (to allow the air in the bag to escape) until the bag is fully submerged. Let the bag soak for 8-15 hours turning it gently every hour or two. Then drain the water from the tub and gently press as much of the remaining water out as possible (never twist or wring the bag). Fill the tub again with warm water and gently work out the remaining soap. Repeat rinsing until the soap is rinsed from the bag. Gently squeeze as much of the water as possible from the bag, then lift it out with both hands underneath. Gently lay it over a wire mesh or other surface where it can drain in a horizontal position in a warm dry place. Do not hang a wet bag vertically. Drying takes 3-5 days.

5
Modern Tents and other Shelters

Each year thousands of nerve-shaken, over-civilized people find that going to the mountains, forests, and deserts is sort of like going home. These areas are useful not only as fountains of timber and water but as fountains of life.
—John Muir

Tents are mainly for protection from the weather. When conditions get worse than you planned, your tent provides the margin. In a tent, the characteristics of basic importance are durability, dependability, internal comfort, and light weight.

Most modern backpacking tents have double roof construction to provide the optimum weather protection. There is the tent's body itself and a waterproof rainfly which stretches over the tent, with an air space between the two layers. The fabric is breathable so that body and cooking vapors can pass through. The waterproof rainfly is vital in summer rains and in winter it helps create an extra layer of warming insulation. If you feel confident it isn't going to storm, you can leave the rainfly behind.

Why not have just one layer of waterproof material instead of a tent with the rainfly added? If the tent was waterproof, moisture created inside could not pass through the fabric. It would condense and create a humid interior. To prevent this, the roof is water resistant, but not waterproof, while the

Figure 5-1. Dome shaped lightweight two person tent, with rain fly added. This tent has a light weight spring metal support structure.

rainfly is waterproof. It should be mentioned at this point that the new product **Gore-Tex** mentioned previously is now being used in the construction of tents. This amazing fiber is both breathable and waterproof. It is possible that the use of Gore-Tex will cause double roof tents to become obsolete in the future.

Typically, the tent floor is made of tough, waterproof nylon similar to the fly except heavier. In many tents, the waterproof floor extends part way up the wall. This keeps ground moisture from absorbing into the lower part of the walls. If the tent is properly designed and pitched, rain will drain off the fly and onto the ground or the lower waterproof portion of the tent walls. In either case, the inside of the tent will remain dry.

In most modern backpacking tents, the roof is made of medium weight, uncoated, ripstop nylon (1.9 oz. per sq. yd.). This tightly woven material is breathable yet resistant to water and wind. It is very strong and durable. Some manufacturers still use cotton poplin which is highly breathable and lighter than nylon. But it is less durable and less resistant to water and wind.

The floor and lower walls are usually made of heavier ripstop nylon (2.5 oz. per sq. yd.) which has a waterproof coating. Most manufacturers make the rainfly of lightweight nylon. This fabric is strong, durable, and slightly elastic.

Ventilation is needed for temperature control. This is accomplished through the door and windows. The openings are usually covered with insect netting with a flap of tent material which can be zipped closed. The various features of the tent should contribute toward overall comfort, and keep out the things you'd like to sleep with the least—rain, snow, and insects.

Shapes and Styles

The selection of a tent that fits your situation leads to the topic of shape and design. This is where tentmakers are concentrating their genius these days. For years the A-shape was the only small tent available. It is simple, low-cost, hugs the ground, and is easily stationed down to withstand the wind. These important features cause it to be popular still among outdoorsmen, but the A-shape is comparatively inefficient in terms of inside space. It tends to make lying down more inviting than sitting or kneeling. Consequently, tentmakers have come up with new suspension systems which create additional inside space. The result is more head and elbow room and more space for storing gear. The new designs are easy to spot. They are any shape except "A". Many of the new designs are dome, or oval shaped, or some modification of these. Just which shape is best is largely a matter of preference.

Forest Tents

There is a large selection of tents made for general use which are referred to as **forest tents**. These tents are designed for use below timberline, where protection from rain, light snow and dew is all that is needed. Forest tents come in various sizes and emphasize different features. Some of the cheaper models are made of a single layer of lightweight water repellent or waterproof material (no rainfly), and they can be purchased for as little as $30.

Conversely, a well-designed, highly durable, free-standing forest tent might cost between $200-$300. A medium quality tent suitable for routine use in moderate weather will cost $75-$150.

Mountaineering (Alpine) Tents

Tents which will be used frequently above timberline or in heavy weather need to be substantially constructed with the best lightweight material available. In some cases, such tents have to withstand long periods of moisture and stiff winds. Under these conditions, an adequate tent is more than a convenience; it can make the difference between tolerable camping and safe camping. Such a tent will have a rainfly over the body of the tent (unless it is made of Gore-Tex) and it might have a tunnel entrance and tunnel vents.

Figure 5-2. Simple two person, lightweight forest tent. Simple two-pole support structure, with no rain fly.

Figure 5-3. Basic two-person tent with a rain fly added.

Cooking inside the tent is sometimes necessary in severe weather. In this event, a vestibule at the tent's entrance and a cooking hole in the floor could be useful. A cooking hole is a piece of the floor, usually two or more feet in diameter, which can be zipped out. This makes it possible to place a hot stove or other cooking items on the bare ground, thus avoiding damage to the floor of the tent. A good quality mountaineer tent will cost $200-$350.

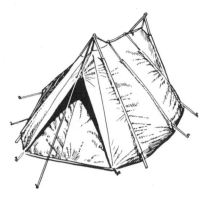

Figure 5-4. High quality mountaineer tent. (Also called an expedition or alpine tent). Designed for cold weather and heavy use.

Tube Tents

Tube tents are light and simple to design. They are used by many backpackers as convenient or emergency shelters. Tube tents are usually made of polyethylene plastic which is windproof and waterproof. The simplest styles are open at both ends and designed mainly for protection from moisture. Some tube tents are enclosed at one or both ends with breathable material.

It's a good idea to mark the bottom of the tent with tape or a felt pen, because the bottom tends to develop pinholes with use. If the tent were pitched so that the floor became the ceiling, these holes could cause leakage. Lightweight tube tents designed for minimal use are quite inexpensive, and they are easy to carry. If you carry one into the outdoors, please bring it back.

Desirable Features

The following features are generally desirable, but not all of these features are necessary for a satisfying experience. The kind of use your tent will receive and the price you can afford will influence which features are included:

● Lightweight in view of the tent's size and quality.

● Maximum usable inside space.

● Tough, waterproof fabric on the floor and part way up the side-walls, with the upper walls and roof made of lightweight breathable fabric and rainfly made of lightweight, waterproof material.

● Windows which open and close from the inside backed with tough sight resistant netting.

- Double seams and durable stitching with strong mildew resistant thread, extra material, and stitching at points of stress.

- Highly durable, two-way zippers with the outside of each zipper covered by a storm flap, preferably elasticized, so that it will stay in place and not snag in the zipper.

- Inside pockets for small items which need to be kept track of and accessible.

- Inside hooks for hanging clothes, lantern, and lines.

- Flame resistant treatment of the fabric and waterproof treatment of seams.

- Grommets which are adequately reinforced with fabric or webbing.

- Collapsible poles made of lightweight aluminum alloy and connected with shock cord to avoid loss and enable convenient assembly. Preferably, poles should be secured into the tent at the base so they will not sink into snow or soft ground.

- Adequate cross ventilation for temperature control and the prevention of condensation.

- Lightweight pegs which are adequate for the particular tent and the conditions under which it will be used.

- A carry bag for the tent and one for the poles and pegs.

In addition, to the above, there are optional features which depend on preference and the kind of use:

- Vestibule or snow tunnel entry, and tunnel vents.

- Cooking hole in the floor.

- Canopy over the entry (on many tents this is included as part of the rainfly).

Important Guidelines
- A potential buyer should give visual and stress inspection of all parts of a tent before buying.

● After purchasing a tent, set it up in the backyard to make sure all of the parts are there and you know how to assemble them with ease.

● Consider whether you would prefer a free-standing stationary tent. The advantage of a free-standing tent is that its location and direction can be changed without disassembling.

● Remember that a taut pitch improves the wind and rain shedding ability of any tent, regardless of its size or design.

● When comparing prices and features of tents and accessories, be sure the same items are included—tent, rainfly, poles, pegs, cord, tent sack, pole and peg sack.

● For backpacking, a good quality two-person tent should weigh no more than four to five pounds.

● When pitching a tent, avoid depressions in the ground which could collect water in the case of rain. Also avoid trenching around the tent because this scars the earth.

● In damp climates or when rain is expected, a ground cloth is recommended underneath the tent floor to add warmth and waterproofing.

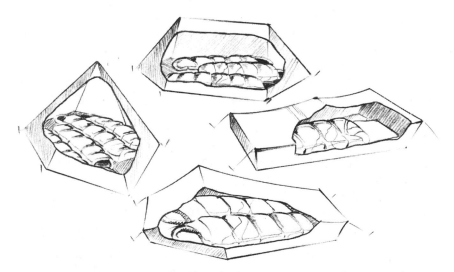

Figure 5-5. Inside space of tents of different shapes and dimensions.

Tent Care and Maintenance

Most of the high quality tents suitable for backpacking are made of a combination of light and medium weight, close knit, nylon fabric with lap felled seams and double stitching with tough, mildew resistant thread. This combination of materials results in good durability and easy care.

- A nylon tent will resist mildew and rot even when stored damp for short periods of time. However, it is better for the fabric to be completely dry. Under no circumstances should a tent be stored for a long period in a damp condition.

- On most tents the thread used for seaming is cotton coated or made of a cotton-nylon combination. It will mildew and rot more readily than the nylon fabric, so it's especially important that the seams be completely dry before the tent is folded and stored.

- Practically all tents have the potential for leaking along the seams due to the stitching if the seams are not waterproofed periodically. A seam-sealer containing a mildew inhibitor is recommended.

- For storage, a tent should be rolled loosely and placed in a cool location free of dirt and rodents.

- Folding the fabric in the same location repeatedly will weaken its water repellency, so this should be avoided.

- An extensive amount of sunlight will deteriorate nylon fabric, so avoid having the tent pitched in a sunny location for a long period. Also avoid flames or intense heat because nylon fabric will melt at about 325°F.

- If a tent is going to stand in place for a long time, the floor should be raised every few days to permit drying. This will prevent mildew and cause less dampness on the inside of the floor.

- If your tent needs to be cleaned, pitch it and sponge it down with warm water and mild soap, then reseal the seams. Avoid machine washing and dry cleaning.

- To protect the floor from punctures and wear, be sure the ground underneath is clear of rocks, twigs, and jagged protusions. Always try to place the tent on a soft, smooth surface. Also, avoid walking on the floor with shoes which have protruding nails or other hard and sharp surface features.

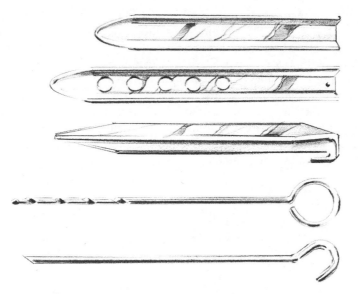

Figure 5-6. Types of tent stakes (T to B): basic aluminum, modified aluminum, plastic power stake, steel screw and steel hook.

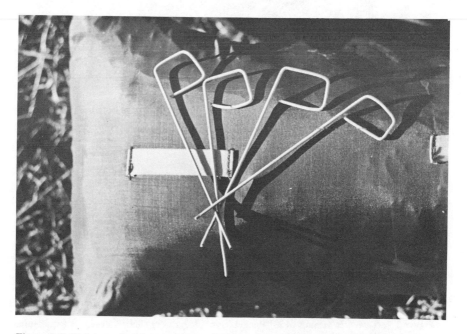

Figure 5-7. Stakes made from metal coat hangers. Large nails can also be used.

Mini-Shelters

Some manufacturers have started producing a sack made of a superior fabric that fits over the sleeping bag and extends beyond the head. It resembles a miniature tent. The discovery of the new, high-quality fabric known as Gore-Tex has expedited the development of mini-shelters. It is certainly a practical idea and one that will probably become popular under relatively mild camping conditions. Figure 5-8 illustrates a mini-shelter. This particular model has a Gore-Tex top for rain protection and breathability, and coated ripstop nylon on the bottom. The head cover can be rolled back, leaving only see-through netting for insect protection. The shelter weighs only two pounds.

Figure 5-8. Gore-Tex "pocket hotel"—ideal for solo backpacking. (Photo use by permission of the Early Winter Co.)

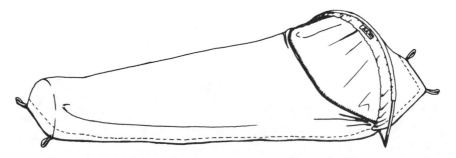

Figure 5-9. A smaller version of a "Pocket Tent" (or a mini shelter) designed for sleeping only, with insect net added.

Tarp Shelters

Camping tarps are usually made of polyethylene plastic (comes in various thicknesses) or canvas, with polyethylene being much lighter and the more popular of the two. A tarp approximately twice the length of the sleeping bag and a couple of feet wider can be used as a substitute for a tent. Place one layer of the tarp under the bag for a ground cloth and bring the other half over the top like a blanket to give protection against wind and rain. This will enable you to sleep under the stars and still have protection from heavy dew and light rain. The disadvantage is the lack of breathability of a tarp. During the course of the night, body moisture will cause some condensation inside the tarp and a small amount of dampness will accrue.

A tarp can be used to construct a simple shelter, sometimes called a lean-to. Also, a more elaborate shelter with side walls can be constructed. All that is needed to make a tarp shelter are two trees, some light rope or cord and pegs—a heavy pole or smooth rocks can substitute for pegs. Also, an A-frame shelter can be easily constructed with a tarp by use of two small tent poles or a line stretched between two trees and some pegs. Carrying lightweight tent poles and pegs is usually an advantage over searching out poles and pegs each time the shelter is contructed. Many hikers prefer four-inch nails or aluminum pegs. These are stronger than wire pegs but they weigh more.

A simple tarp shelter gives adequate protection from vertically falling rain and the accumulation of dew. Its advantage are low cost and light weight, but it has obvious limitations.

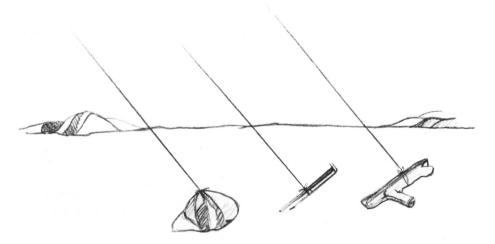

Figure 5-10. When pitching a tent on snow or loose soil bury the stake (center) or substitute with a buried stick (R) or rock (L).

Emergency Shelters

Sometimes a cave, rock crevice, or overhang is available when emergency shelter is needed. Other possibilities include protection underneath a large evergreen tree or deadfall. On occasion a lean-to constructed from natural material can be justified. But for reasons of environmental protection, such shelter should be constructed only in emergency, and then it should be dismantled after use.

Figure 5-11 illustrates a variety of lean-to styles. By studying the figure you can see the parts that are needed and visualize variations of the basic design. The most essential characteristics are: (1) It must be sturdy enough to support its own weight plus force from wind, rain or snow; and (2) The material on the roof should be placed in a shingle-like manner to enhance the proper drainage.

Side walls are optional but they are a distinct advantage in bad weather. Also, a tarp can be hung from the support pole to provide a front wall which can be opened and closed.

Figure 5-11. A variety of lean-to styles can be easily be constructed with a tarp or a plastic sheet.

6

Lightweight Stoves and Firemaking Techniques

The absolute freedom of the backpacker gives every hour an intense lucidity.

Today there are many places in national forests and parks and near population centers where outdoor fires are not permitted. However, in some locations there is still enough freedom and firewood to enjoy the comforts of an evening campfire. In some locations, permits are needed, and in all locations it's important to conserve wood and to follow safety practices. The hiker should look upon a fire as a luxury, not a necessity. A well informed outdoorsman can get by nicely without one.

Camp Stoves

Why carry a stove? What's wrong with going hobo or Daniel Boone style—doing your cooking over an open fire with a fry pan or dingle stick. Some of the reasons are: (1) growing scarcity of firewood; (2) more restrictions due to fire hazards; and (3) greater concern for the natural environment. Furthermore, it's more enjoyable to cook with an efficient camp stove that smokes not, heats yes, and weighs very little. It's cleaner, quicker and more ecologically acceptable.

Today's outdoorsman can choose from an array of camp stoves. We have stoves that burn alcohol, butane, propane, kerosene, or white gas. There are differences in shape, size, weight, safety features, dependability, and of course, price. The selection of a stove should ultimately be influenced by the amount and kind of use. Price certainly should not be the main factor, because with a cheap product, you often pay a big price later in inconvenience and repairs.

Alcohol stoves are clean burning, but they are relatively inefficient. Insulation against wind is a necessary precaution, and this retards vaporization of the alcohol and results in less heat and slower cooking. The alcohol is burned in an open cup where little control can be maintained over the flame. Some models use a simmer ring which does permit a measure of control.

Butane stoves work on the vapor principle, and butane vapor burns cleanly. It vaporizes at 32°F (0°C). This means it can be encased in a relatively light, metal container, but it also means that when the temperature goes below freezing, butane gradually becomes more useless until finally at cold temperatures it becomes a self-defeating experience. Obviously, a butane stove is unsatisfactory for cold weather camping.

Propane burns just as cleanly as butane and much more efficiently. Propane vaporizes at much lower temperatures, -50°F at sea level. So it requires a container made of stronger material than for butane. This added weight is a negative factor for the backpacker. Propane ignites easily and it's relatively safe. Because of its convenience, many backpackers use propane in spite of the fact that the combination of stove and cartridge are relatively

Figure 6-1. Optimus 8-R gas stove, weight 23 oz.

heavy. Ecologically oriented hikers will always carry the container both ways, even when it's empty. Leave footprints but not empty cartridges.

Kerosene stoves are not very common in the United States. In Europe and Asian countries, kerosene is much more plentiful. There is an objectionable smell to regular kerosene; however, an odorless kerosene is now available. If you're planning to hike in foreign countries, want an added factor of safety, and are interested in a slight economical advantage, kerosene may be the way to go. But most backpackers in America consider a kerosene stove to be a weak choice.

White gas stoves are the most popular. They are clean and efficient and the fuel is readily available. When backpackers speak of white gas, they do not mean automobile fuel. This fuel will burn, but it gives off dangerous fumes and will soon foul up the stove. They mean Coleman fuel, the recommended fuel which can be found from coast to coast in a variety of stores. White gas stoves generally have one fault—they create a hot spot in the center of the pot, and constant stirring of the contents is necessary to avoid burning. One way to get around this is to place a round of tin (from a #2 can or larger) between the flame and the pot, thus spreading the heat. Should you for some careless reason run out of Coleman fuel while cooking, be sure to allow the stove to cool before opening the fuel cap. Otherwise you might become part of the fireworks display.

Figure 6-2. Stove made from a tin can, to use with canned heat.

Weight of the stove is important, since it will be carried on your back. Remember that the total weight includes both stove and fuel. A light stove which requires a quart of fluid weighs more than a heavier stove which burns for hours on a cupful. The table which follows includes interesting information about weight, dimensions, burning time and other characteristics of popular camp stoves. This will be helpful in selecting the right stove for your particular use.

Figure 6-3. Hank Roberts mini gas stove. Weight, 17 oz.

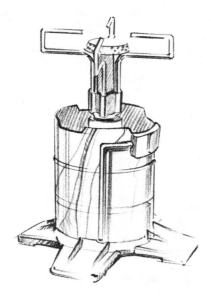

Figure 6-4. Bleuet S-200 butane stove. Weight, 26 oz.

Stove Model	Fuel	Weight ounces Full	Empty	Fuel Capacity (Ounces)	Full Throttle Running Time (hrs/min.)	Height (inches)	Width or Diameter of Base (inches)	Pot Support Width (inches)	Set-up Time (min/sec)	Time to Boil (min/sec)	Approx. Cost
Peak 1 #576	Gas	42	32	10	1:30	6½	3-7/8	4½	1:30	7:30	$40
Peak 1 #400	Gas	38½	28½	10	1:25	6¼	3-7/8	4½	1:30	7:30	35
MSR-G	Gas	33	18	15	1:20	4	3	7	5:35	5:05	75
MSR-GK	Multi-fuel	33	18	15	1:20	4	3	7	5:35	5:20	80
Optimus 8-R	Gas	26½	22½	4	1:10	3¼	5	5	1:55	8:45	45
Optimus 88N	Gas	25	21	4	1:05	5¼	5½	5½	2:00	8:50	45
Optimus 111-B	Gas	68¼	53¼	15	2:10	4	6-3/4	3½x6	1:50	5:50	75
Phoebus 625	Gas	47	32	15	2:35	7¼	4-7/8	6½	1:35	6:25	50
Phoebus 725	Gas	32	24	8	1:15	4½	4-7/8	5½	1:35	6:35	55
Svea 123R	Gas	22	17	5	1:00	5¼	3-3/4	5	1:35	6:20	40
Optimus Purist 1	Gas	28	22½	4	:52	4½	4½	4½	1:00	6:50	50
Bleuet S-200	Butane	27	16	11	1:30	4½	3½	3½	1:30	5:20	20
Primer G.H.	Propane	74	62	12	2:00	11	3	3	2:00	6:30	25
Primus 71	Gas	22	12	10	1:20	4½	4¼	6½	1:40	6:20	30
Baby Ender	Gas	31	21	10	1:30	4	3½	6	1:30	6:40	30

Table 6-1. Selected backpack stoves and their characteristics.

Auxiliary Equipment and Supplies

Auxiliary equipment for camp stoves includes a cook set, funnel, and fuel bottle. These items should be carefully selected so they fit your needs well. The Optimus mini-pump for Optimus stoves is certainly useful because it conserves fuel and contributes to cleanliness. Also, the Optimus mini-oven, which works well with all stoves, ought to be considered.

There are several good cook sets available. One of the best is the Sigg-Tourister which fits the Svea 123 stove. The Tourister provides its own wind screen, two pots, and a fry pan with a lid which can be used for heating or serving. There is a cheap, Taiwan-made replica of the Swiss-made Sigg set. Get the real thing because the cheap replica is often a source of trouble.

A fry pan lined with Teflon will save a lot of needless scrubbing. Carry a nylon cleaning pad and enjoy the fruits of technology.

The new mini-oven made by Optimus makes cooking on the trail fun—casseroles, french bread, baked desserts, etc. With this oven, there's no need to confine yourself totally to dehydrated and freeze dried products. Trail meals can become something better than bare necessities.

Extra fuel should be carried only in leakproof, light, metal containers. Fumes and odor from fuel carried in the pack can easily contaminate camping supplies, particularly food. In view of this, food should be carried as high in the pack as possible with the stove and fuel in the lower compartment or side compartment and wrapped in polyethylene.

For safety reasons keep extra fuel a safe distance from the stove. Treat the fuel in the same manner that highly flammable materials should always be treated. Be absolutely sure the flame is out and the stove is cool before replenishing the fuel supply.

Figure 6-5. Light weight containers for extra fuel: aluminum (L) and fiberglass (R). It is helpful to carry a cap with a built-in pouring spout (available at most outdoor equipment stores).

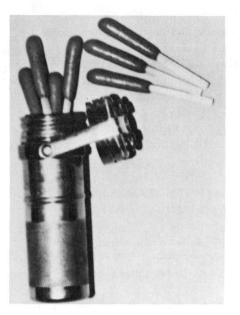

Figure 6-6. Waterproof match container and waterproof matches.

Campfires

An open campfire can add greatly to an evening in the outdoors, and often the day seems incomplete without one. But the well-informed backpacker knows where and when an open campfire is appropriate and how it should be done.

There are three elements necessary to produce fire: **air, combustible material,** and **heat** to start the burning process. In severe weather, the only practical way to start a fire is with matches or a lighter (always backed up with a supply of matches). However, starting fires by primitive methods such as flint stone, bow drill, or optic device is possible under favorable conditions by one knowledgeable about such techniques.

A candle ought to be part of the equipment of every outdoorsman. It can be ignited under extreme weather conditions, even if it gets wet. You can depend on it for both light and heat inside a shelter as well as an aid for making fires. In addition, it can be put out and relit several times, and the life of a candle is long when compared with other firestarts, not to mention its low cost.

> A TWO INCH SECTION OF THICK CANDLE CAN SERVE WELL AS A FIRE STARTING AID IN ADDITION TO OTHER USES.

71

Here are some important guidelines to remember when building a fire:

● Have an ample supply of matches, and keep them completely dry by carrying them in **waterproof** containers. Have two containers in case one becomes lost. Some campers choose to waterproof each match by dipping the head in melted paraffin wax or fingernail polish. Also, waterproof matches can be purchased in many outdoor equipment stores.

● Do not waste matches by trying to ignite improperly prepared tinder. The tinder should be bone dry, carefully prepared, and sufficient in amount.

● Carry a fire-making aid to conserve your match supply. The butt of a candle an inch and a half or more in diameter is the best.

● Remember that split wood burns better than whole chunks.

● Soft wood is easier to start, but hard wood burns longer.

● Keep an adequate supply of wood under shelter from wet and storm.

Tinder, Kindling, and Fuel

Tinder comes in many forms. Some of the more common forms are twigs, dry branches, dry grass, weeds or moss, and dry bark from certain trees and shrubs. In the winter, shavings from dry branches or shredded bark are the best possibilities. Look for completely dry, highly flammable material, and take what time is necessary to locate and prepare an effective bundle of tinder. In many locations the best source of tinder is the reddish brown branches of evergreens where porcupine or beaver have injured the tree or killed certain branches. These highly flammable needles are known as "indian kerosene." They are filled with dry pitch and seem to explode when a flame is put to them.

The most difficult circumstances under which to find suitable tinder are following heavy sleet or rainstorms or in areas where the humidity is very high. Under these conditions, practically all materials are damp, and the best possibilities are the underneath layers of bark or thick moss, combined with the shavings of dry twigs and branches.

It is a good idea to watch along the trail to determine the kinds of fire material available in the area so that, when it comes time to make a fire, you already have the best plan in mind. Like many outdoor methods, successful fire-making under adverse conditions depends upon whether you have adequate knowledge, and are alert and perceptive to the particular circumstances.

Figure 6-7. Two kinds of the fire making tinder: twigs (top) and bark (bottom).

Kindling comes in the form of larger twigs and branches which will become ignited readily from the heat of the tinder. Be sure to have on hand a sufficient amount of well-prepared kindling, and have ready access to a supply of **larger fuel.**

Some conservationists recommend that kindling and fuel be gathered from the ground as much as possible, and that hikers avoid breaking dead branches from trees or pushing over dead trees.

The dry tinder should be packed tightly enough to let the flames spread easily, but not so tight that the flame suffocates due to lack of air. An adequate supply of oxygen is essential.

First-small pieces of kindling and then larger pieces should be carefully placed in strategic locations over the tinder, letting the flame build from the smaller to the larger pieces. Once the larger pieces are burning well, maintaining the fire with dry fuelwood is a simple matter.

Primitive Fire Making Methods

The best way by far of being certain that you are prepared to start a fire is to have an adequate supply of matches in waterproof containers. However, you might someday find yourself in an emergency situation where you will need to resort to a primitive method, or you might choose to experiment with the following methods just for the interest of doing so:

● **Flint and Steel**—A steel knife blade or a file struck against hard stone will cause sparks. If the sparks are cast into very dry and fine tinder, smoke and smoldering will occur. When this happes, blow on it gently with short puffs until the tinder bursts into a flame. Charred cloth or very fine steel wool, if you happen to have it, will ignite even quicker than the finest of tinder.

● **Magnifying Glass**—A strong magnifying glass (or a lense from certain flashlights) placed in the direct sunlight so that a point of light is focused into dry tinder will cause the tinder to smoke and eventually break into flame. Again, charred cloth or steel wool will enhance the technique.

● **Bow Drill**—This apparatus sometimes offers the greatest chance for success. It has four parts: a **fire board,** a **socket** and a **bow.** The **fire board** should be at least a half inch thick and large enough to form a suitable base. A slab of cottonwood, pine, or aspen will do. A depression large enough to fit the drill is made close to one edge. A few strokes of the drill will smooth and deepen the depression. A notch is cut in the side of the board so that it reaches the center of the depression. This notch catches the fine powder ground by the drill and it is in this powder where the spark will eventually ignite.

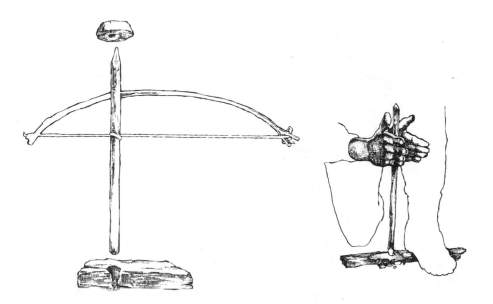

Figure 6-8. Illustration of a bow drill firemaking apparatus (left) and a hand drill (right). A camper should not depend on these methods unless he/she is experienced in using them.

The **drill** is made of piece of dry willow-type wood 12 to 15 inches in length. It should be flat on the bottom and round on the top. The **socket** is made by cutting a depression the size of the drill in a piece of wood, bone or rock that fits the hand. For this piece, the harder the wood, the better. Place some kind of grease in the pit of the socket for lubrication.

The **bow** should be of stiff, willow-type material 18 to 24 inches long, preferably with a fork at one end. The string can be made of nylon cord or leather. A heavy shoelace is sometimes substituted successfully. Fix one end so that it can be loosened or tightened as needed to cause proper functioning.

To use the bow drill, the fire board is placed on a flat piece of bark or wood with well-prepared tinder very close by. The sparks will fall onto the piece of bark or wood where it can quickly be placed in the tinder. You might prefer to have the tinder placed where the spark will fall directly into it.

The proper position for working the drill is to get down on one knee and place the other foot on the fire board to hold it steady. The socket is pressed downward with one hand, and the drill, with the bow cord wrapped once around it, is pressed downward into the fire board socket. The bow is pulled

Figure 6-9. Illustration of igniting fine tinder after hot dust from a bow drill has been cast into it.

back and forth smoothly in a sawing motion until the drill tip begins to smoke. Gradually spin the drill faster and press harder with the socket until black dust begins to collect in the notch and there is more smoke. When it seems certain there is enough heat for a spark, lift the drill away and fan the dust lightly. If there is a spark the dust pile will begin to glow, then carefully place it in the tinder and blow it into a flame.

7

Food and Cooking Arrangements

There must always be wilderness, a desirable someplace for young spirits to discover the wonders of nature and our dependence upon it.

For the backpacker, the selection and preparation of food can be one of the truly enjoyable experiences. Keep in mind that backpacking is hard work so you need a nourishing diet. You will want foods that are tasty, and your selection should represent a good balance of substantial foods to which you are accustomed. This will minimize the risk of indigestion. Also keep in mind that when backpacking, you use many more calories per day than normal. An average size man engaged in light work uses 3,200 to 3,500 calories; the same person hiking several miles up and down slopes with a 30-pound pack can use 4,500 to 5,000 calories

Most foods carried on your back should be in the form of dried, dehydrated, or freeze-dried foods. It is not practical to carry foods which contain a high proportion of water. Consider that a #2 can of peaches weighs 30 ounces, while a freeze-dried package of peaches, which will provide the same amount of food, weighs only 2 ounces. A quart of whole milk weighs 32 ounces, while enough powdered milk to make a quart weighs only

2½ ounces. Two cans of vegetable soup weighs 22 ounces while an equivalent package of dehydrated soup weighs 2 ounces. The list could go on and on. With proper planning a backpacker can eat as well on the trail as he can at home. Meals on the trail should be as close to what you usually eat as possible.

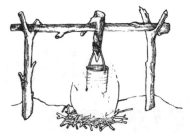

Figure 7-1. Crossbar kettle hanger for heating water or cooking food.

Dried and Dehydrated Foods

A good variety of dried and dehydrated foods can be found in almost any grocery store. They are less expensive than freeze-dried foods and they are easy to prepare. Cooking these foods on the trail is often no more difficult than the cooking you normally do at home. The following is a list of most of the **dried** and **dehydrated** foods worth considering in your backpack menu. A good variety of substantial foods from this list is recommended.

Grains
Instant oatmeal (packaged with sugar and spices added)
Cream of wheat or cream of rice
Granola or granola bars
Wheat germ (honey can be added)
Rice, instant
Spaghetti, macaroni and noodles
Packaged macaroni and meat dinners, and noodle dinners
Dried Soybeans
Pancake, ready mix
Biscuit mix (can be cooked on a stick)

Meat and Dairy Products
Beef or venison jerky
Dried beef (chipped)
Salami, pepperoni, summer sausage
Dried bacon
Powdered milk
Dehydrated eggs (including ham, bacon or cheese mix)
Instant gravy

Figure 7-2. A dingle stick and tin can pot for cooking over open fire.

Fruit and Vegetables
Dried apples, apricots, peaches, pears, prunes and raisins
Frozen fruit juice concentrate (a variety of kinds)
Dried potatoes (powdered)
Dried peas and beans (for soups)
Dehydrated soup mixes (a variety of kinds)

Sweets, Nuts and Desserts
Granulated sugar (can be added to a number of foods)
Hard candies
Chocolate bars
Energy bars
Shelled nuts (walnuts, almonds, peanuts, cashews, brazils)
Jello and pudding mix

Beverages
Instant hot beverage mixes
Bouillon cubes
Lemon or orange powder (such as Tang and Kool-Aid)
Cocoa mix, Ovaltine, or Postum
Jello (as hot drink)

Miscellaneous
Food sticks or food bars
Salt & pepper
Dehydrated onions

DEHYDRATED PACKAGED FOODS ARE ESPECIALLY USEFUL BECAUSE OF THEIR SMALL AMOUNT OF WEIGHT AND BULK.

Freeze-dried Foods

Freeze-drying is the best method of preserving certain kinds of food. While many foods lose taste and color through the drying or dehydration process, much of the original color and taste is retained through freeze drying. The disadvantages of freeze-dried foods are that they are relatively expensive, and they are more bulky than dehydrated foods. If your finances will permit only minimal freeze-dried foods, consider meats first because these are much superior to dried meats and much lighter than regular meat. Also, freeze-dried fruits are a nice convenience for which there is no good substitute in dehydrated form.

Freeze-dried food products include: meat, poultry, and fish; fruits of various kinds; a variety of vegetables; and several desserts. Following is a fairly comprehensive list of particular dishes that are available. Some are available in compressed form which causes them to be very compact:

Combination Dishes
Stews of various kinds
Meat and rice
Spaghetti and meat sauce
Chili and beans
Chop Suey
Beans and franks
Macaroni and cheese
Lasagna with meat sauce
Casseroles of various kinds

Breakfast Courses
Omlettes of various kinds
Eggs with mcat of various kinds
Granola with fruit
Buttermilk pancakes
Hashbrown potatoes
Cornbread or muffin mix

Meats
Beef—ground or steak
Ham, sausage or bacon
Chicken or turkey
Pork chops
Beef jerky
Shrimp
Meat balls and sauce

Vegetables
Green peas
Green beans
Carrots
Corn
Potatoes

Fruits
Apples
Bananas
Strawberries
Pineapple
Peaches
Pears

Other dishes
Soup—various kinds
Pudding—various flavors
Ice cream—various flavors
Beverages—orange, lemonade, chocolate, and coffee

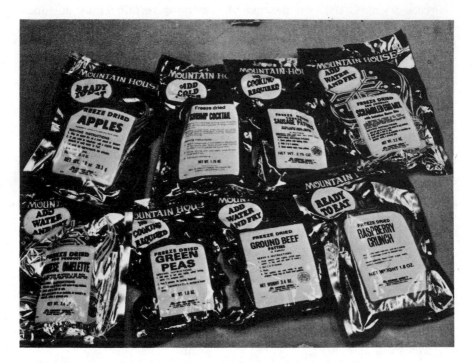

Figure 7-3. There is a large variety of tasty freeze-dried foods available. They are light and easy to prepare.

Trail Snacks

Backpackers usually like to carry snacks in their coat pocket or the side pockets of their packs to munch on along the trail. If done within proper limits, this can provide needed replenishment of energy, but it can be overdone to the point that you lose your appetite for a good meal. Also, too much rich food between meals can cause indigestion. The following are useful ideas for trail snacks:

- Roasted soybeans
- Granola
- Beef jerky
- Hard candy
- Chocolate bar
- Salami, pepperoni, or summer sausage
- Dried fruits (apples, appricots, peaches, raisins, etc.)
- Energy bar
- Shelled nuts
- Sunflower seeds
- Freeze dried fruits (eaten dry)

Total Weight

If you are careful in the selection of food, staying as much as possible with dried, dehydrated, and freeze-dried foods, you can get by just fine on about two pounds of food per day. If you plan with extreme care, you can live on 24 ounces.

Small plastic (polyethylene) bags are handy for packing individual food portions. The ziplock type is very handy. The smaller bags of food each meal can be placed in one larger bag so that you have a separate bag of food for each meal. In turn, the three meals for a particular day can be packed in a large bag.

> **FOOD CAN BE PACKED IN PLASTIC BAGS FOR SEPARATE MEALS. THIS ENHANCES PLANNING AND FOOD PREPARATION.**

Breakfast

A good breakfast is vital to the backpacker. Try a combination of these dishes to get off to a good start at the beginning of each day:

Cereal—instant oatmeal with sugar or honey added, or if you prefer cold cereal try granola or grape nuts with honey and milk.
Pancakes—with syrup, honey, or jam.
Hash—made with dehydrated potatoes, dehydrated eggs, dried onions.
Bacon and eggs—dehydrated eggs with dried bacon mixed in.
Drink—make the hot drink of your choice, or cold fruit juice using juice concentrate.
Fruit—If you like fruit for breakfast try a package of freeze dried peaches or pears, or maybe you would prefer dehydrated prunes or apricots.

Lunches

On most occasions you will find a cold lunch satisfactory, and you ought to consider such things as bread sticks with chip beef or salami, dried fruit or freeze dried fruit, nuts, cheese, peanut butter and honey mix, and lemon or orange Tang to drink.

However, if you decide to go for a hot lunch you can set up your single-burner stove and prepare a combination of the following:

Hot soup—made from packaged dehydrated soup
Fresh fish—if you happen to be fishing in the area
Macaroni—made with a macaroni and cheese mix
Beef stew—made from a freeze-dried stew mix
Vegetable salad—made from freeze dried vegetable salad
Drink—hot or cold, as you choose
Dessert—a combination of dried fruit, nuts, and candy

Dinner (Supper) Ideas

If you have spent most of the day on the trail, this will probably be your biggest meal, but still you should not stuff yourself. It is better to eat three meals per day of fairly equal size than to deprive yourself at breakfast and lunch and eat too much at night. Consider a combination of these dishes for dinner.

Hot biscuits—using pop-out biscuit mix or powder mix   cooked on a stick.
Meat—freeze dried chops, steaks, or hamburger patties.
Stew or mulligan—made from a freeze-dried package, or by mixing together dehydrated soup, dried onions, and bacon chips.
Mashed potatoes—dehydrated.
Vegetable of your choice—freeze dried.
Beverage—Hot jello or some other nourishing hot drink.
Macaroni, spaghetti, or noodles.
Rice—with raisins, sugar, and spices added.
Dessert—it is a good idea to save the dessert for a bedtime snack. Consider dried fruit and nuts, freeze-dried fruit, freeze-dried pudding, or candy.

Cooking Arrangements

It is interesting and fun to try different methods of cooking, especially over an open fire or in hot coals. Here are some attractive ideas.

Figure 7-4. Trout cooked over an open fire with a willow and tin foil cooking device.

Bacon on a Stick

If you choose to take a chunk of bacon, the bacon strips can be cooked to a tasty flavor by wrapping the bacon around the end of a stick two or three feet long and holding it over the coals in much the same way you would to roast a hot dog. Be sure the bacon is wrapped securely around the stick.

Bread on a Stick

Pop-out biscuit dough is ideal for wrapping around a stick and baking over coals. It is especially good while warm, with jam or honey. This is the most tasty bread that can be prepared on a camping trip, and it is ideal for winter backpacking. Bread on a Stick can also be prepared by mixing Bisquick with water and molding the dough over the end of a fairly large stick.

Camp Stew

Tasty camp stew can be made by starting with a package of dehydrated vegetable soup and adding to it such things as noodles, dried beef, bacon, diced pieces of salami, dried peas, dried onions, bouillon cubes, etc.

Baked Fish

A whole trout or other such fish can be baked by placing it directly on top of coals that are not too hot and turning it as needed to keep it from burning. After the fish is cooked, peel away the charred skin, add salt and other seasoning as desired, and the fish is ready to eat.

Aluminum Foil Cooking

A number of individual foods and combinations of foods can be packaged in foil and baked over coals. For example, corn on the cob or potatoes can be roasted, or meat and fresh vegetables, such as hamburger, carrots, and potatoes can be packaged together and baked to make a sort of stew. Also an improvised fry pan can be made by stretching foil around the fork of a stick, with a handle about two feet long.

Meat on a Spit

Meat of various kinds such as chicken or a chunk of beef or venison can be cooked to suit your appetite by rotating it periodically, or at a steady slow rate, over hot coals. The spit can be constructed by spanning a long slender stick between two forked uprights, or by having one slender stick propped diagonally in the fork of a single upright similar to a dingle stick.

Paper Bag Cooking

Surprisingly, foods that have a sufficient amount of moisture in them can be cooked inside a substantial paper bag. For example, you can mix dehydrated eggs with bacon in a small, well-made paper bag and actually cook it over coals that are not too hot. You can do the same with dehydrated potatoes, or with biscuit dough, or with any other food that is not too liquid or too dry. The key to this kind of cooking is to have a paper bag that is substantial, and to cook food that is moist enough to keep the bag from burning, but dry enough not to soak through the bag, and to cook over coals that are not too hot.

Figure 7-5. Bacon cooked over an open fire on a stick.

Figure 7-6. Bread on a stick over an open fire.

Figure 7-7. An egg can be fried on a hot rock.

Figure 7-8. Meatloaf or vegetable & meat stew can be cooked in tin foil over coals.

Living off the Wild

When you want to add some special interest to your diet, try some of the foods available in the natural environment. Look closely and you'll find that the woods resemble a smorgasbord and it's all yours for the taking. Not all the useful ideas could be included here because there is a large variety of natural food in any particular setting and the kinds of edibles vary in different geographic areas, but a few ideas can give you a starting point and possibly stimulate your interest and creativity. Consider these possibilities.

Fresh Salads

By taking along some salad dressing, you can create a tasty salad by selecting some of the following plants and putting them together in the right combination—water cress, Indian lettuce, calamus stalks, dandelion greens, barbarea, lily buds, violet blossoms, tips or buds of wild roses, young cattail stalks, wild artichoke, wild onions and wild garlic.

Fruits

There are a rather large number of fruits available in different localities in season. The more common varieties are strawberries, blueberries, raspberries, huckleberries, serviceberries, elderberries, wild grapes, chokecherries, wild plums, and currants.

Grains and Seeds

Various grains or grass seeds are available in late summer and autumn which can be eaten raw or boiled or mixed in soup. Included in this potentially long list are the following—bluegrass, bristlegrass, pear grass, rice grass, nannagrass, amaranth (hickweed), wild rice, goldenrod, wheatgrass, bluejoint grass, and quackgrass.

Greens and Stalks

The leaves and stalks of numerous plants can be cooked in boiling water for a prescribed period of time and eaten. Often these plants are more tasty when smothered with butter and seasoning. Consider these possibilities—dandelion crowns, dandelion greens, poke sprouts, infant cattail blooms, young cattail stems (interior portion), barbarea, asparagus, lily buds, bracken fern, bulrush stalks, burreed stalks, groundsel, storkbill or heron's bill, artichokes, lamb's quarter or goosefoot, mallow or cheeseweed, nettle or stinging nettle (young plants), purslane, samphire, dock plant, rhubarb, young thistle plants, umbrella or stroup plant.

Figure 7-9. Bread can be toasted by holding it close to hot coals.

Edible Roots

A large number of roots are edible, either raw or cooked by boiling or baking. Usually they need to be cooked for a relatively long time. Among the more useful edible roots are the following—balsalm root, biscuit-root, Indian potato, waterleaf root, violet or dogtooth root, yampa or carroway, bulrush root, and burreed root.

Meat Sources

Perhaps some of the following sources of meat would be available and would catch your fancy—crayfish-boiled or deep fried; frog legs-boiled, roasted or deep fried; turtle soup or boiled fresh water mussels, or fish.

Miscellaneous

Potentially available food sources not included in the above are wild garlic (for flavoring), wild mushrooms (be sure you can identify the poisonous varieties), wild onions or onion greens—raw or in soup-and sassafras (for making tea).

Cooking and Eating Utensils

This is one aspect of backpacking where some people get carried away and take more than is needed, but perhaps not more than is preferred. For **cooking,** one person can get by fine with a small fry pan and a large metal cup which can be used both as a pot for heating liquids and for drinking. If

Figure 7-10. A compact cook set for two people: open (L) and closed (R).

there are two people, a larger fry pan, and a medium size pot for cooking will be needed. The exact number and the specific cooking utensils are a matter of preference, depending on one's style of living while on the trail.

In terms of eating utensils, all one person needs is a cup, a dish or plate, a spoon and a camper's pocket knife. If a cup has measurement marks, it can serve a double purpose as a measuring cup in food preparation. A shallow bowl or curved dish is better than a flat plate. However, a plate is acceptable if it has a turned up lip around the edge.

From the standpoint of weight, either plastic or aluminum is preferred. Aluminum utensils have the advantage of withstanding direct heat from the fire, while plastic has the advantage of more appeal to the touch of most individuals, especially when the weather is cool. The final choice is a matter of preference. Self-sealing plastic bags can be used as mixing bowls for batter, salads, etc. They are easy to clean and easy to carry. Some individuals like to take a small wire grill for open fire cooking.

Figure 7-11. Many backpackers prefer only a small pan and a plastic cup.

Figure 7-12. Convenient combination set of eating utensils. Some backpackers prefer sturdy plastic utensils.

Water

It is very important in planning your day-to-day route to keep in mind the various sources of water. Unless you know the route well and are familiar with the water supply, you will be wise to carry ample water in a canteen. Whenever you establish camp, it's a good idea to be close to water because this makes camp life cleaner and more enjoyable.

In determining whether a source of water is safe to drink, check on whether there is water life in it. Water devoid of life should be highly suspect. The water in most high mountain streams and springs is drinkable. Almost any water is drinkable in small amounts if properly treated. So if there is any question as to the water's purity, boil it or apply a water purification treatment. In cases where the water is possibly not pure and you are unprepared to purify it, avoid drinking it and thereby avoid possible intestinal infection.

Figure 7-13. Water containers which fit in a pack: three sizes of plastic bottles and an aluminum container.

A COLLAPSIBLE PLASTIC WATER BAG THAT CAN BE HUNG FROM A BRANCH IS THE NEXT BEST THING TO HAVING A FRESH-WATER SPRING RIGHT IN CAMP.

8
Useful Backpack and Camping Techniques

Outdoor activity is essentially a renewing experience—a refreshing change from the domestic routine.

This chapter includes extensive information that hopefully will help make your backpack trip more enjoyable and safer.

Walking Techniques

Walking with a pack on a wilderness trail is not vastly different than walking on a city street. However, there are a few tips about technique which can lead to the conservation of energy and a more enjoyable trip.

If the weather is hot, **get up early** and put some miles behind you during the cool morning hours. Your body will use less water and less energy in the cool temperature. Also, early morning and dusk are the best times to see wildlife. Many animals and birds feed at these times and rest during the hot part of the day.

If you are hiking with a group, the person setting the pace should **be sensitive** to the hiking ability and conditioning of the others. A fast hiker who is too impatient should arrange a place and time of rendezvous and go

95

> **INTERESTED IN KNOWING JUST HOW FAR YOUR WALK? WEAR A PEDOMETER ON YOUR BELT AND ADJUST IT FOR YOUR OWN STRIDE.**

ahead. He should not force everyone to travel at his pace. However, this same rule does not apply to a slow hiker. Never desert a slow hiker assuming that he will catch up later.

The pace should be rhythmic and steady. An erratic pace is inefficient. Remember that more energy is used per distance at a fast pace than at a slower pace. Running or trotting is very poor use of energy and should be strickly avoided except in emergencies when speed is necessary.

Walking **up and down hills** is very inefficient as compared to walking on the level. Therefore, in selecting your route avoid unnecessary changes in elevation. Also, try to select a route that will avoid rocky surfaces, deadfall, heavy underbrush, and wet terrain.

The true test of your conditioning is **when you have to climb.** Backpacking uphill is one of the most strenuous aspects of outdoor activity. A slow and steady pace will pay off here. On very steep grades a method called the **rest step** can be used. It is done by pausing at the completion of each step with the weight of the body carried on the back leg which is locked at the knee. Then another step forward is taken, followed by a pause. Traversing a steep grade is usually better than going straight up.

Walking **downhill** with a heavy pack consumes less energy than going uphill. But unless the proper technique is applied, it can be very hard on the joints. It is important to cushion the impact with just the right amount of joint action at the weight bearing phase of each step. In other words, do not lock the joints as they bear weight. On occasion, hikers have the problem of the toes jamming against the ends of the boots. This can be remedied by tightening the lower half of the boot laces and tying them at the half-way point, then lacing the top half with a normal amount of tension. Sometimes wearing an extra pair of socks will help, and driving with less force downward onto the foot will also help.

It always adds to a trip to arrange your **rest stops** at scenic locations or where there are features of special interest. Why not make your resting time count by adding enjoyment and interest to your experience.

Figure 8-1. A hiker taking an easy pace at a high altitude.

Crossing Streams

Crossing streams with a heavy load on your back is quite a different challenge from crossing without a pack, and many sad tales could be told about this. The weight of the load makes it much harder to balance and the chance of getting hurt if you fall is greatly increased. You must be especially cautious on slippery rocks and on rocks which provide small or unstable footing. If you cross on a pole or log, be sure it is strong enough and is not cracked or rotted; also beware of knots and slippery spots.

When you face a hazardous stream crossing, first analyze all of the possibilities in terms of location and methods. After you have made a decision, improve the crossing area as much as possible with available rocks and deadfall. Then consider potential aids such as tree branches which you can hold for balance, a balance stick if the stream is shallow enough to use one, or a handrail that can be formed by lying a pole across the stream at the right height. If you wade across, face diagonally downstream from the current so, if you fall, you will go forward.

If you're going to cross on a pole or log, it is sometimes an advantage to remove the pack from your back and carry it in front of you in a low position just barely above the walking surface. In this position it can be used as an aid in balance. If the pole is high enough above the water, you can reduce the hazard by straddling the pole and working your way across in this position. Under some circumstances you might consider hanging the pack underneath the pole by looping a rope attached to the pack around the pole and then working it along in front of you as you move across the pole in the straddle position. Remember these points:

● If there is much chance of getting your clothing or equipment wet, it is much better to walk a distance to a bridge or other suitable crossing.

● Do no make hasty decisions about crossing a stream. Study the situation carefully and be sure you make the best decisions relative to both location and method.

● Be especially cautious of slippery or unstable rocks, rotten or broken logs, swift water, and deep holes.

● If you cross with the pack on your back, be sure to unfasten the waistbelt so that the pack can be quickly removed in case you fall into the water.

Leadership on the Trail

If you are the leader of an organized group going on an extensive backpack trip, your general objective should be to minimize hazardous and unpleasant experiences and maximize safety and enjoyment. Leadership needs vary considerably with different groups and circumstances. Larger groups and less experienced members require closer supervision and better direction.

If you are a leader, you ought to make yourself thoroughly acquainted with the route and related conditions such as potential hazards, weather, sources of water and food, and rescue procedures. Select an assistant who is qualified to take charge in your absence.

One important role is to help decide who should go on the trip, giving consideration to each one's experience and preparation, physical condition, attitude toward the activity, and compatibility with other members. In terms of needed equipment, you should consult with the others to be sure they know what equipment each one should take. Be sure all party equipment is obtained and properly packed.

Here is the checklist of some of the more important responsibilities of the leader:

● Plan and arrange transportation to and from the point of departure.

● Obtain whatever permits are necessary for access and fire making.

● Keep current on weather conditions.

● Make sure you have a reliable compass and map.

● Provide adequate orientation to the members and to any others who would be concerned about the group's whereabouts and safety.

The group leader plays a key role in route selection. To the seasoned outdoorsman, it is obvious that the shortest walking distance between two points is a straight line. But the route must often be altered to suit the irregularities of the terrain and to avoid hazards. Generally, it is a good idea to follow a route that leads through relatively open country and one that is as level as possible. Unnecessary climbing up and down hills should be strictly avoided because this is a great waste of energy.

Sometimes you might choose to deviate from an otherwise desirable route to avoid hazards or to arrive at certain points of interest. The route should be designed to avoid heavy brush, dense woods, and fallen trees. Also stream crossings must be considered.

It is the leader's function to organize the group for travel. He should command the pace, remembering that it is better to travel at a slow and steady pace than to go too fast and have to rest often. However, occasional rest periods are desirable to break the monotony and provide an opportunity to adjust equipment and converse with each other.

Another leadership function is to manage the party equipment. You should follow a plan for having items carried by different group members, and have the items rotated among members as often as necessary. Be especially sure that party equipment is not inadvertently left at a rest stop or campsite due to a misunderstanding of who should carry it.

During rest stops and also while in camp, it's a good idea to plot your position on a map and orient yourself thoroughly to terrain characteristics and any special landmarks. Educate other members about these matters so they are well informed and become accustomed to orienting themselves. Try to help the group recognize and enjoy the scenic and unique feature of the area.

JERKY, DRIED FRUIT, MIXED NUTS OR GRANOLA MAKE GOOD TRAIL SNACKS.

Trail Courtesies

There are a few basic courtesies that every hiker should know and apply.

- One of the unwritten laws is that you always help another backpacker who is in difficulty. Even though it might be inconvenient, it's an obligation and should not be neglected.

- When hikers who are traveling in opposite directions meet, those traveling uphill should step aside and make way for the downhill travelers. This is because those traveling downhill will be moving faster and have less need of a rest. When passing a hiker moving in the same direction, it's a courtesy to ask for the trail. The one being asked should yield by stepping off to the right, unless it would be better to move to the left for safety reasons.

- Never litter along a trail and if someone else has been so discourteous to do so, you ought to dispose of the litter.

● Never discard useless equipment at a campsite or along the trail. Carry it out so that it can be properly disposed. Be especially sensitive about following proper sanitary procedures so that you will not detract from someone else's experience. Be particularly protective against the contamination of water.

● Select a campsite which is not too close to other campers. One reason for going out of doors is to get away from groups of people and crowded conditions.

Route Planning and Trail Marking

Even though the authors are advocates of freedom and flexibility in one's schedule, it is recommended that you have a **basic plan for each day**, including the approximate distance you will travel, the route you plan to follow, and approximately where you will camp. Let the appropriate person back home know of your overall plan. If you become detained or change plans, try to send information back home by some method.

In view of the emphasis on environmental protection, **trail marking** by individuals has become a questionable practice. Cutting marks on trees with a knife or hatchet or squirting spray paint on trees and rocks are **unacceptable** practices. If for some reason it's necessary to mark a trail, the use of small strips of colored crepe paper or cloth tied to branches in strategic locations is the preferred method. These markings are relatively undistracting to the environment and they disappear in a short time. The U.S. Forest Service and National Park Service sometimes use trail numbers. For example a trail known as #16 will have a small sign every so often to mark the trail. It would be very poor judgement and discourteous for a backpacker to remove or damage any official trail marker or direction sign.

THE USES TO WHICH A BANDANNA CAN BE PUT ARE NUMEROUS. SOME OF ITS MORE COMMON APPLICATIONS ARE: (1) FOREHEAD SWEAT BAND: (2) NECK SUN PROTECTOR: (3) HANDKERCHIEF (TIE ONE END TO YOUR BELT RATHER THAN STUFFING THE WHOLE THING INTO A POCKET); (4) UTENSIL TOWEL: AND (5) WATER FILTER.

Campsite Selection

It is important to plan the day's travels so the party will arrive at a desirable campsite early enough to prepare camp before dark. There are certain characteristics that are important in a campsite. Among them are the following:

1. Avoid natural hazards such as possible rock slides or dead trees that might fall over.

2. Select an area that offers ample protection from wind or cold.

3. Availability of drinking water is an important consideration. You ought to camp conveniently close to the supply but not so close that your activities contribute to water contamination.

4. An adequate supply of firewood is important. If open fires are to be built, the wood from most dead trees is satisfactory if it is dry (see the chapter on fires).

5. Suitable locations to place shelters is another important consideration and the exact kinds of shelters to be used might influence the campsite selection. If tents are used, a site is needed that provides suitable locations for an adequate number of tents.

6. Scenic features of the site should be considered because enjoyment of the scenery is often one important purpose of the trip.

7. A route of retreat should be kept in mind so that it would be convenient to move out toward home in case of inclement weather or other emergencies.

KEEP YOUR TENT AND SLEEPING GEAR CLEAN BY REMOVING SHOES BEFORE ENTERING. IN FAIR WEATHER YOU CAN LEAVE SHOES OUTSIDE; OTHERWISE PUT THEM IN A PROTECTIVE PLASTIC BAG AND BRING THEM IN.

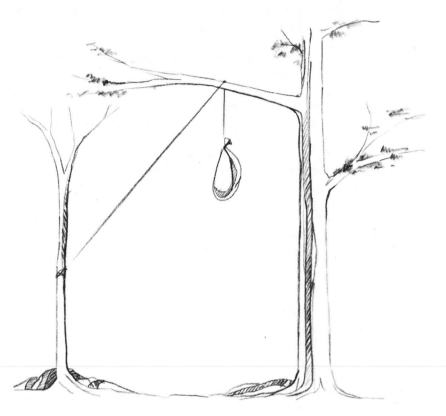

Figure 8-2. Suspending your supply of food from a tree branch will protect it from bears and other animals. The bag ought to be no less than six feet from the tree trunk, five feet from the branch, (bottom) and ten feet from the ground.

Responsibilities in Camp

The leader is supposedly the most knowledgeable member of the party about hiking and camping techniques; thus, he should exert his leadership in the following areas:

● Coordinate the placement of individual camps or shelters.

● Advise the party members about the best placement of fires.

● Casually examine each camp for safety hazards, giving special attention to unsafe fire arrangements and misuse of dangerous equipment such as a knife, hatchet or ax.

103

- Advise party members as needed on the storage and care of food and water especially in view of the presence of animals that might be attracted by the food.

- Be sure that appropriate sanitary conditions are provided and proper procedures followed.

- Try to prevent night hikes away from camp of the kind that might result in someone becoming injured or lost.

- Encourage party members to practice good outdoor ethics in connection with each other and with the environment.

Once the trip is over, the leader has the responsibility of making certain that all equipment is returned to its proper place, that injuries are reported to the right sources, and that all those concerned are informed of the completion of the trip.

Other Important Considerations

Knowing Your Equipment

If you're a beginner, there's no better place to become accustomed to backpacking than in your own backyard. It's a convenient place to practice packing and unpacking your gear, hoisting your pack, and making sure that all parts of it fit properly. This same kind of useful experimentation should be done with your tent, bedroll, footwear and stove.

Permits and Permissions

In some areas, such as national or state parks, **permits** are needed in order to camp or build a fire. Obviously, it is important to obtain the appropriate permits in order to be legal and to know the restrictions under which the area may be used.

Furthermore, it is sometimes necessary to obtain **permission** to **trespass** on private property. If the owner willingly gives permission, you should feel fortunate. If he shows resistance, you should assume there are reasons for it. Perhaps the reasons relate to lack of consideration by previous backpackers. You ought to make sure that you don't contribute to a problem for those who will seek permission in the future. In other words, be highly considerate of the property and the owner.

Pack Animals

Occasionally, it's an advantage to take a **pack animal** (horse, burrow, or dog). In areas where this is acceptable, the use of a horse or burro makes it possible for individuals to carry lighter loads. Also, having such animal can provide a transportation advantage in case a member of the party becomes injured or ill. The disadvantages are: (1) acquiring an animal and the needed packing equipment; and (2) taking care of the animal while on the trip. A few individuals have robust dogs which they like to take along for company and to assist with the packing of gear. However, in many hiking areas dogs are not permitted. Dog packs can be acquired at certain outdoor equipment stores.

Belonging to a Group

Many backpackers find extra enjoyment in belonging to an **outdoor organization** where they meet people and participate in activities of mutual interest. There are many small organizations of this kind on college campuses and in communities. In addition, there are such national organizations as the Wilderness Society, the Sierra Club, and the Appalachian Club. Every serious backpacker ought to consider the extra enjoyment that would come from membership in one of these organizations.

Figure 8-3. In potentially hazardous situations, good equipment and proper techniques are especially important.

9

Routes, Orientation, And Navigation

Each mountain, forest or river is a world of its own, unique in pattern and personality.

There are no infallible laws governing a backpacker's choice of route because each area has its own peculiarities of geography and terrain. On different occasions and in different locations you might find yourself in terrain with broad, open valleys skirted by massive mountains, or in narrow canyons walled by steep rocky slopes, or in rolling hills with indistinct features, or in heavenly vegetated canyons. Route selection is obviously influenced by the characteristics of the area.

An experienced outdoorsman is usually aware of important guidelines in route finding, and by knowing any outdoor area well he knows something of all outdoor areas. However, there is no substitute for first-hand experience in a particular geographic location, and even the wisest traveler should enter each new area humble in spirit.

Knowing Direction

Nature offers several useful direction indicators, and in many cases nothing more is needed. But it is important to recognize the margin of error in direction indicators and not place too much confidence where the potential error is large.

In all parts of the United States the **sun rises** somewhere between the east and southeast and sets in the west. During winter months the sun's position is slightly south of its position during summer. Its deviation to the north reaches the farthest point in late June, and its deviation to the south is greatest in late December.

The **south slopes of mountains** are sunnier, and are therefore usually drier than the north slopes. The vegetation on the south is sparser and sometimes of a dryer variety. North slopes are snowier, and often steeper and more rugged because of more glaciation in past ages. The old idea that moss grows on the north side of trees and rocks is more often true than not. But, this is not a highly reliable direction indicator.

On a sunny day, direction can be determined quite accurately by **using a watch**. When the time piece is layed flat and turned so the hour hand points to the sun, true south lies halfway between the hour hand and twelve o'clock.

> **AT ANY TIME OF THE YEAR, IN THE NORTHERN HEMISPHERE, THE SUN IS GENERALLY SOUTH OF YOU, A GOOD COMMON-SENSE INDICATOR OF DIREC-TION.**

Compass Use

In cases where exact directions are needed, there is no substitute for a reliable compass because it is the most accurate method of establishing direction. The usefulness of a compass is increased considerably by a good map.

A compass is a magnetized needle mounted so that it can respond freely to the earth's magnetic force. Regardless of one's geographic position, the needle of the compass always points to the magnetic north pole (in the northern hemisphere), unless there is some distraction in the environment which interferes with the natural magnetic field. On very rare occasions such distraction may come in the form of large bodies of iron ore or certain rock formations. In addition, some items of equipment might be slightly magnetized such as a hatchet, metal cookware, a wristwatch, belt buckle, etc. It is important to keep the compass clear of these distractions during use.

The compass needle does not point to the geographic north pole (the earth's north axis), but rather to the magnetic pole which is approximately 1,000 miles south of the geographic pole. This is not a very important consideration when only general directions are needed, but this difference must be taken into account when you want to orient yourself exactly and locate your position on a map.

A substantial, inexpensive compass ($8-$10) is adequate for most purposes. The north end of the needle ought to be distinctly marked since confusing north and south, as can be done under certain conditions, would produce gross error. A device for locking the needle in position is useful because it prevents oscillation while reading the compass and protects the compass from excessive wear from movement while being carried.

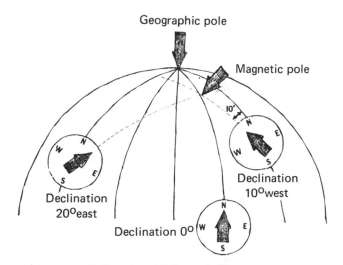

Figure 9-1. The relative position on the earth of geographic or true north as opposed to magnetic north. A compass is attracted to magnetic north while the grid system on which maps are based is laid out on true north.

Maps and Map Reading

If you are planning to tour through country where you are unfamiliar with the routes and landmarks, you will want to have a map which is accurate and provides sufficient detail.

Until a few decades ago, maps were prepared almost entirely by ground survey; walking over the terrain, taking compass bearings and elevation angles, and measuring distances by rod and chain. However, today surveyors need only to walk over enough ground to establish a few key distances and elevations. With this information and aerial photographs, machine-made maps are constructed which are nearly perfect representations of the face of the land.

Figure 9-2. A quality compass with attached base plate and straightedge. This kind is especially valuale for orienting a map, taking a field bearing and following that bearing.

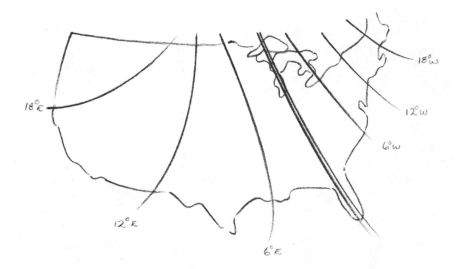

18°W
18°E
12°W
6°W
12°E
6°E

Figure 9-3. Degrees of inclination from magnetic north at various points in the United States.

Backpackers find uses for maps of different complexity and precision. In some cases you will need only a sketch made by a friend. In another case you might want to obtain a map which has been recently prepared from aerial photographs and is almost incredibly precise. But whatever the case, it is imperative that the map be adequate to fill the particular need at that time.

Pictorial Relief Maps. These maps are drawings of the landscape from a particular angle. They show the relative elevations and terrain characteristics. Relief maps are usually constructed from topographic maps, and even though they are not three-dimensional, the three-dimensional illusion is given. They cannot be used effectively for compass navigation.

Topographic Maps. This kind of map, which gives a symbolic picture of the lay of the land from directly above, is widely used by backpackers. Topographic maps made during the last two or three decades by government agencies have been constructed from aerial photographs and are highly accurate. To be certain that the map is reliable look for the following identifying phrase on the map, "topography from aerial photographs by multiplex methods."

The Geological Survey maps are published in four scales, referred to as series. The ideal scale of the outdoorsman is the "fifteen minute series."

City map at 1:12,500 scale.

Figure 9-4. Sample maps: relief map (above) and topographical map (below).

111

These maps are constructed on a scale of 1:62,500 (roughly one inch to the mile).

If you can read a topographic map well, it's like having an aerial photograph in front of you. It tells almost everything you need to know about the terrain.

> **WHEN A SERIES OF CONTOUR LINES ARE CLOSE TOGETHER, THE TERRAIN IS STEEP. WHEN THE LINES ARE FAR APART, THE TERRAIN IS GENTLE.**

Reading a Map. Official maps are constructed with the top of the map pointing toward geographic north. The map is layed out according to the grid system, and the grid lines converge at the north and south geographic poles. Since maps are oriented to geographic north, and a compass points to magnetic north, there is a difference known as the **magnetic declination.** On **official** maps the magnetic declination is usually indicated, and it is expressed in degrees. An explanation is given later of how to deal with this difference.

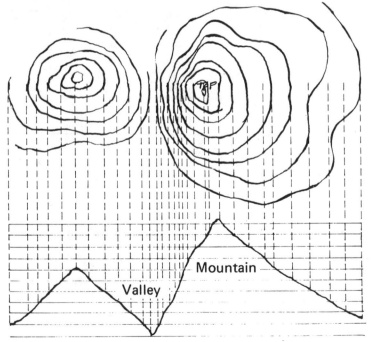

Figure 9-5. Illustration of the meaning of contour lines on a map.

112

Topographic maps show the shape of the terrain by use of contour lines. These lines represent elevations from sea level. On a particular map the elevation interval between contour lines is always constant and it is expressed in feet. This means the closer the contour lines the steeper the terrain. For convenience in reading, usually each fifth contour line is heavier and its elevation is given. After you have had some map reading experience, contour lines take on great meaning. For example, circles indicate a summit. A series of "V's" or "U's" leading into the circle indicate a canyon or a draw. "V's" or "U's" pointing away from the circle indicate a ridge. Lines that run together indicate a cliff, while lines spread far apart mean the area is relatively flat.

Since the contour lines show elevations and thereby indicate mountains, gulleys, cliffs, and plateaus, a person can determine the kind of terrain where his route will lead him. Sometimes this can save hiking many miles only to find that the route leads to an impassable canyon, cliff, or peak. Also, the contour lines can help select the most uniform route and this will save time and energy.

On an official map, black indicates man-made objects, including roads, buildings, trails; blue represents water—rivers, creeks, lakes, etc.; dark green indicates forests; light green represents shrub and grass areas; tuffled light green indicates marshes or swamps; red is used for division boundaries and the more important roads; and the contour lines are brown.

> **STAYING ORIENTED IS AN IMPORTANT SAFEGUARD AGAINST BECOMING LOST.**

Orientation

By the orientation procedure you find your ground location. If location cannot be determined by visual examination of the area, then resort to the use of map and compass. First orient the map to the land, knowing that the top of the map points to geographic north unless otherwise indicated on the map. In order to orient the map truly, the magnetic declination for that particular geographic area must be known. Usually this is indicated on the map, and sometimes members of the party will know from past experience the declination for that particular region.

Lay the compass on the map and align the north-south grid lines of the map with the needle of the compass (magnetic north). Then rotate the map and compass as a unit toward the geographic pole by the amount of the magnetic declination. For example, if the magnetic declination is 15 degrees right (east), align the map with the magnetic pole, then rotate the map and compass to the left until the needle of the compass points to 15 degrees. The grid lines would then be aligned with the geographic pole, and the map would lie true to the land.

The next step is to spot two or more characteristics of the land which you can identify on the map, or vice-versa. It is preferable to select characteristics that are generally on different sides of you in order that you can determine accurately your position relative to those points. Peaks, lakes, streams and cliffs are often easy to identify.

After you have identified two or more points on the map, connect the points either by drawing a line with a pencil or placing a straight edge connecting the points. You have then established a **line** position. By use of the line and further study of the points in relationship to your position, you can establish your point position. Once you have this, it is a good idea to trace your route along the map as you move in order that your point position is always known.

THE U.S. GEOLOGICAL SURVEY PUBLISHES A SHEET DEFINING ALL SYMBOLS USED ON THEIR MAPS. IT'S WORTH HAVING.

Land Navigation

While traveling, your view of the country is constantly changing. By maintaining a sharp eye on your surroundings you can keep constantly updated. Each time a prominent characteristic is observed, you should identify it on the map and relate your position to it.

If you are an experienced outdoorsman, you know that country looks amazingly different from the back view than the front view. Therefore, glance over your shoulder often in order to register in your mind the appearance of the land when approaching from the opposite direction. This practice is especially important if backtracking becomes necessary. Plant in your mind the back view of prominent points such as after crossing a stream, when departing from a lake, after passing a cliff, coming out of a canyon or at points where trails merge.

When there are no obvious landmarks, or when landmarks are obscured by fog or darkness, it might be necessary to mark the return route. (This should be avoided unless there is special reason to do it). Probably the most acceptable method is to use colored crepe paper cut in thin strips and tied to trees and brush at intervals along the trail. This material is durable enough to last several days even in stormy weather, but perishable enough to vanish in a reasonable time. As mentioned before, this is much better than cutting marks on trees or spraying paint on trees and rocks, methods which are unacceptable in view of the emphasis today on environmental considerations.

> **AN ALTIMETER SHOWS ELEVATION, GIVING YOU A THREE-DIMENSIONAL CONCEPT OF YOUR LOCATION.**

Actions When Lost

An expert outdoorsman will not remain **lost** but, having learned humility, he should always practice wise preventive measures and be prepared with sufficient food and supplies in case he becomes **detained**. Caution combined with alertness, good judgment, and ample information about the area can reduce to a bare minimum the chance of becoming disoriented.

However, if you should become disoriented, the first thing to do is **stop**. Take all the time you need to collect your thoughts, gain full composure, thoroughly analyze your situation and think through all the alternatives. Then force yourself to **take a little more** time just to be sure that you are fully collected and are not rushing into a wrong decision.

The first action to consider is **backtracking**. If you know that you were correctly oriented a short time earlier, the safe thing to do is backtrack to your last oriented position and get a fresh start from that point. If your last point of orientation is too far, or if for some other reason you cannot backtrack, the next best alternative is to **establish camp**, and give yourself a day to study the situation.

If becoming reoriented seems quite hopeless, you might choose just to **stay put** until help arrives. This decision would have to be based on a knowledge of the particular circumstances. Another possibility is to **move cautiously** ahead watching very carefully for landmarks that could help you become reoriented. It is wise not to follow this procedure too long or too far, but sometimes it is worth experimenting with for a short distance. Another alternative, but usually a last resort, is to **establish a base line** leading to a route of sure return to safety, such as a highway or a river. A baseline is a straight line that can be established by use of a compass. For example, if the map shows or if you otherwise know that there is a north-south highway which runs along the west slope of a mountain range in which you are located, you could use your compass to determine west and then follow that line (base line), checking your direction often with the compass. You will eventually arrive at the highway. Also by having a general concept of the drainage system of the area you can follow stream beds and know where this will lead you. A good point to remember is always go downward, not upward.

Calmness, careful **analysis** and an **unhurried approach** are your best friends when you are lost, while **panic** and **hurry** are your worst enemies. If you are an experienced outdoorsman, and if you use good judgment, you can live in the wilderness for several days. During that time you can certainly figure out a sensible solution to the problem of being lost. If it is likely that companions or rescuers will search for you, it would be much better for them if you stay put. During the waiting time it is beneficial to think positively and keep yourself in good spirits. Remember these rules:

- A clear and cool head will usually find the best solution.

- Stop, sit down, and try to figure out where you are. Use your head, not your legs.

- If caught by night, fog, or a storm, make camp in a sheltered spot. Build a fire in a safe place. Gather plenty of dry fuel.

- If injured, choose a clear and obvious spot and make a smoke signal.

- Don't panic, don't run, don't worry, and above all, don't give up.

Orientation and navigation in the wild country involves both an art and a science. Some people have the gift to do it well, but all can learn the tools, and everyone can improve with practice. It is an exciting part of outdoorsmanship because it is an interesting challenge that the terrain presents to you.

Sources of Maps

Some of the best maps available for all regions of the United States can be obtained from the U.S. Geological Survey. Maps of areas east of the Mississippi River, including Puerto Rico and the Virgin Islands, should be ordered from the **Branch of Distribution, U.S Geological Survey, 1200 South Eads Street, Arlington, Virginia 22202.** Maps of areas west of the Mississippi River, including Alaska, Hawaii, American Samoa, and Guam, should be ordered from the **Branch of Distribution, U.S. Geological Survey, Federal Center, Denver, Colorado 80225.** Standard quadrangle maps published in the 7½ - or 15-minute series are priced at $1.25 per copy. Prepayment is required and the money must accompany each order. Payment may be made by money order or check payable to the Geological Survey. The price includes surface transportation for areas within the 50 states and other possessions of the United States, Canada, and Mexico. A map should be ordered by name, series, and the state in which it is located. Upon request, the Geological Survey will furnish an index of the available maps of a geographic area, and from this index you can select the particular maps you want. In addition to the standard quadrangle maps mentioned above, the Geological Survey offers state base maps in black and white ($1.50), and multi-color ($2.00), county maps, and national park maps. Topographic maps of areas of Canada can be obtained from the **Map Distribution Office, 615 Booth Street, Ottawa, Ontario, Canada.**

Maps of United States forest areas may be obtained from regional and district offices of the U.S. Forest Service. National park maps are available at the headquarters office of each national park. Outdoor equipment stores sometimes have adequate maps. Other sources of maps are listed below. The maps from these sources are less official than government maps, but frequently they are useful for backpacking in a particular locality.

- Adirondack Mountain Club, 172 Ridge Street, Glensfalls, New York 12801.

- Appalachian Mount Club, 5 Joy Street, Boston, Massachusetts 02108.

- The Appalachian Trail Conference, 1718 "N" Street N. W., Washington, D.C. 20036.

- Greb Hiking Bureau, 1 Adam Street, Kitchener, Ontario, Canada.

- Green Mountain Club, 108 Merchant Row, Rutland, Vermont 05701.

- Mazamas, 909 N. W. 19th Ave, Portland, Oregon 97209.

- New York-New Jersey Conference, GPO Box 2250, New York, New York 10001.

- The Sierra Club, P.O. Box 7959, Rincon Annex, San Francisco, California 94120.

- Wilderness Society, 729 15th Street, N. W., Washington, D.C. 20005.

> TO PROTECT YOUR MAP, YET
> HAVE IT USABLE AT ALL
> TIMES, KEEP IT FOLDED INSIDE
> A CLEAR PLASTIC BAG.

Care of Maps

There are several ways maps can be protected while in the field and it's worth doing. The U.S. Geological Survey is planning to produce pocket-sized, folded editions in plastic jackets just for hikers and other outdoorsmen. Several outdoor supply houses provide plastic cases in which a folded map will fit. Also, plain old sandwich bags can be used. The U.S.G.S. suggests laminating your map to a sheet of muslin. This makes a nearly indestructable product.

One of the very best methods is the application of self-adhesive material (one brand is Con-Tact A-21). Cut two adjacent quadrangles into convenient pocket-sized rectangles (about 5 inches by 5 inches for 15-minute quads) and glue the pieces back to back. Carefully position the pieces on a sheet of adhesive plastic leaving about 1/4 inch between the squares. Do it carefully because the adhesive sticks immediately. Then with equal care complete the sandwich with a second sheet of plastic so that the quads are enclosed between the plastic sheets. Rub firmly to remove air bubbles and trim the edges, leaving a small margin of plastic. The folds will occur at the quarter-inch spaces between the quads, and repeated folding will eventually crack the plastic. The cracks can be repaired easily and permanently with fiberglass filament tape. Protected in this manner, maps will never get soggy and they'll wear for a long, long time.

The Future of Map Making

The U.S. Geological Survey, the main supplier of high-quality maps, publishes some 30,000 topographical maps of the United States and sells about 11 million copies each year. In addition to outdoorsmen, the maps are used by engineers, surveyors, land planners, developers, railroad personnel, and local governments—virtually everybody with a need for reliable information about the lay of the land.

Recent word from the U.S.G.S. is "metrics." Some of the first metric maps are already in print—part of the series that will cover the Lake Placid area of New York, home of the 1980 Winter Olympics. If the new metric maps continue to follow the Lake Placid pattern, they will be different in several ways in addition to the unit of measurement:

Scale. The metric scale will be 1; 25,000 rather than the common 1; 24,000 or 1; 62,500 (one inch to the mile) now used.

Coverage. The coverage will be twice the area of the 7-1/2 minute maps today; 7-1/2 minutes of latitude north and south, and 15 minutes of latitude east and west.

Symbols. Highways, buildings, and other features will be represented by new symbols that be can be read by computers as well as people.

Is all this better? Some say no—they couldn't care less about metric maps but, on the other hand, there are many explorers and world travelers who backpack and these people would like to have an element of consistency among maps produced in different countries. The metric system offers that.

10
Backpacking For Fitness

One of the most basic things that can be done to improve physical fitness is to encourage the simple pleasures of walking and hiking.

One of the greatest needs of Americans today is more participation in vigorous activities. Backpacking can be one of those activities. It is well established that walking one or more miles a day can improve the physical conditioning of many adults, especially those who are middle-aged and over. Obviously hiking several miles a day up and down slopes can have a positive influence on the physical fitness of even the young and vigorous. When a 20 to 40 pound pack is added, the overload on the body systems becomes even greater and the result is improved fitness.

Backpacking can be as strenuous as you are willing to make it, and strenuous activities provide overloading of body systems. This causes the systems to develop to higher levels. The one disadvantage of backpacking is its sporadic nature. Some people go backpacking infrequently, and if this is the case the fitness program must be supplemented by other activities between trips. But for one who backpacks frequently, the trips certainly make a significant contribution to fitness. Some interesting comparisons are given in the following table about the relative exercise of hiking as compared to other activities.

Table 10-1. Calorie Expenditure Per Minute for Various Activities

	Body Weight							
	90	108	125	143	161	187	213	240
Walking (3.0 mph) (level)	3.4	4.1	4.9	5.6	6.2	7.5	8.6	9.3
Hiking, 40 lb pack, 3.0 mph (level)	5.2	5.4	6.0	6.8	7.7	8.9	10.1	11.4
Snowshoeing (2.5 mph)	5.4	6.5	7.5	8.6	9.7	11.2	12.8	14.4
Mountain Climbing	6.0	7.2	8.4	9.6	10.7	12.5	14.3	16.0
Skiing (cross country, 5 mph)	7.0	8.4	9.8	11.1	12.5	14.6	16.6	18.7
Running, 8.5-min. mile, (7 mph)	8.4	10.0	11.7	13.3	14.9	17.4	19.8	22.3
Running, 7-min. mile, (9 mph)	9.3	11.1	13.1	14.8	16.6	19.3	22.1	24.8
Running, 5-min. mile, (12 mph)	11.8	14.1	16.4	18.7	21.0	24.5	27.9	31.4

Physical Conditioning

Because backpacking is very strenuous, one who is not physically prepared to handle it subjects himself to: (a) possible inability to keep up with his companions; (b) severe discomfort from overwork; and (c) possible physical harm if he works harder than the body systems are prepared to handle.

One important approach to the physical conditioning problem is to **keep your physical fitness at a fairly high level** constantly. For many backpackers, the activity is seasonal, and during the off season one's state of conditioning will deteriorate unless other forms of activity are substituted. This is exactly what ought to be done. Jogging, calisthenics, bicycling, and regular participation in vigorous sports will help keep your level of fitness where it should be. Then when the next backpacking season comes around, you will be ready.

Endurance Development

Physical conditioning for backpacking is largely a matter of developing endurance. Endurance is the ability to resist fatigue and to recover quickly after fatigue. Actually there are different forms of endurance known as **muscular** endurance, **cardiovascular** endurance, and **total body** or general endurance. Backpackers need to be concerned with all of these forms of endurance.

All of the systems of the body adhere to the **law of use** in a manner exactly opposite to mechanical devices. The body systems grow and develop with use, while machines wear out with use. Conversely, the body systems deteriorate in the absence of use.

121

The **law of use** implies that **muscle endurance** will increase with constant use of the muscles, and if endurance is to improve very much, the muscles must be worked consistently beyond previous levels (overloaded). Actually, the best way to develop muscle endurance for a particular activity is to participate extensively in the activity itself, or an activity similar to it but more strenuous. In the absence of adequate muscular endurance, the muscles fatigue and rest is required. Often muscle cramps are brought on by muscle fatigue.

For the backpacker who carries a heavy load and hikes long distances, all of the major muscle groups need to be well conditioned. Obviously the muscles are of particular importance.

A reasonable level of **cardiovascular endurance** is necessary for the muscles to continue to function. The individual muscle cells must receive nutrients and oxygen from the cardiovascular system which also transports waste products from the muscles. The respiratory system supplies oxygen to the circulatory system and receives carbon dioxide and other waste material from it. If the circulatory system fails to keep the muscles adequately supplied with oxygen and nutrients and free of waste products, fatigue occurs. Cardiovascular endurance is dependent upon regular, high-level use of the cardiovascular system. This can occur only by exercising the large muscle groups to the extent that heavy demands are placed on the circulatory system. In other words, vigorous exercise which causes the heart to beat faster and stronger and which causes breathing to become faster and deeper promotes cardiovascular endurance. If this kind of overload is applied regularly, the cardiovascular system will improve or at least maintain its level of fitness. In the absence of such stimulation, the system will gradually deteriorate. Running is one of the best activities for building cardiovascular endurance.

Total body endurance is related to the efficiency with which the body is able to do work and the ability to replenish the supply of energy as it becomes depleted during work. Here again, the **law of use** applies. A person who works the body at a high level regularly will have a higher state of fitness. This condition will cause him to utilize more efficiently, and the energy production processes will be more effective. Remember, as far as the body's systems are concerned "that which is used regularly will be ready for use, while that not used will not be ready."

Diet

In addition, total body endurance is related to diet, both content and amount. A supply of body sugar (glucose) is necessary in order to constantly replenish body energy. Carbohydrates are converted to glucose more readily than fats or protein. This is the reason that candy, honey and other sugar-laden foods provide a ready lift when one begins to feel tired and depleted. It is a good idea, however, to not depend too much on quick

Figure 10-1. Long distance running (jogging) is an excellent activity for backpackers to maintain conditioning during the off-season.

replenishment of energy through consumption of sugar sweet foods. This can result in a feeling of nausea and indigestion. Under heavy work conditions, the diet should be well balanced, but with emphasis on energy rich foods (carbohydrates). Included in the carbohydrates are the various grain and cereal products, vegetables and fruits, in addition to the sugar-laden foods.

Body Weight

Another important consideration is **proper body weight.** Fat is non-working tissue, which in fact is nothing more than dead weight. It must be carried and it must receive a constant supply of oxygen and nutrients transported by the blood. Therefore, an abnormal amount of fat is very undesirable under conditions of heavy physical stress. Vigorous exercise and overweight are incompatible.

People who are serious about maintaining proper weight need to be knowledgeable about the facts involved. Body weight fluctuates on a temporary basis as a result of perspiring, but this does not cause a loss of real weight. It is only a loss of body fluids which are soon replaced through the normal processes. **Real body weight** is lost or gained through a change in the amount of body tissue, and this is caused by a differential in the amount of kilocalories consumed and the amount utilized. A pound of fat is equivalent to approximately 3500 kilocalories. This means that if you were to eat 3300 kilocalories of food each day and expend 3200 kilocalories, your net surplus would be 100 kilocalories. In 35 days, you would accumulate 3500 extra kilocalories or approximately one pound of body weight. It is by this slow process that many people gain weight during seasons when they are less active. Of course the reverse would happen if you were to consume 100 less calories per day than you expend, and this is what often happens during the seasons when backpackers are active.

Muscle Soreness

Muscle soreness can be a problem to a backpacker who has not conditioned himself sufficiently. Two forms of soreness can occur:
1. Immediate—where pain occurs shortly after heavy exercise and passes quickly.
2. Delayed—localized soreness which appears 12 to 24 hours after exercise.

Immediate soreness results from a combination of the passage of potassium across the muscle cell membrane into the tissue space, and the sudden accumulation of acid waste products following heavy muscular work. The pain occurs soon after exercise and the person recovers from it rather quickly.

Delayed muscle soreness is not so transient and the pain sometimes per-

Figure 10-2. Developmental exercises are especially valuable which add strength and muscular endurance to the leg and back extensor muscles. These are the muscles that do the majority of the work in hiking and supporting a pack.

Figure 10-3. Fat is non-working tissue, which in fact is nothing more than dead weight.

sists for several days. Apparently this form of soreness occurs from a combination of the following: (a) the accumulation of metabolites; (b) the onset of fatigue of muscle tissue; and (c) possibly the rupture of muscle fibers.

Relief of prolonged soreness can be enhanced by three techniques:

● Mild, smooth exercise which does not contribute to additional soreness, but does increase circulation in the sore muscles.

● Holding the muscles in a mildly extended, semi-relaxed position for short periods of time.

● Massage, which helps to remove waste products faster than normal and causes the muscles to feel loose and relaxed.

Effects of Elevation

As a person ascends to higher and higher altitudes, the total pressure of the atmosphere decreases because of the decreased weight of the column of air above. Since the percentage of each of the gases in the atmosphere remains the same regardless of altitude, the partial pressure of each of the gases decreases proportionate to the total pressure decrease. This means that the density of oxygen becomes less with increased altitude.

A constant supply of oxygen must be furnished to the tissues of the working muscles in order for them to continue at a sustained rate. Under conditions of heavy exercise at high elevations, the supply of oxygen delivered to the working muscles sometimes becomes inadequate and this results in fatigue. Even though the potential supply of energy in the body is adequate, it cannot be converted efficiently to energy in the absence of oxygen. This is why people's ability to perform in vigorous endurance activities gradually diminishes with increased altitude.

To give some meaningful comparisons which illustrate the problem, consider the following. At sea level the oxygen pressure in the interior of the lungs is 104 milimeters. At an elevation of 10,000 feet it is reduced to 64 milimeters and at 20,000 feet, it is less than 40 milimeters. Luckily, the

> **AT HIGH ALTITUDE HARD WORK TAKES ITS TOLL DUE TO LESS OXYGEN IN THE AIR. SPECIAL CARE MUST BE TAKEN TO AVOID OVER EXERTION AND ALTITUDE SICKNESS.**

oxygen saturation of the blood drops considerably less than the pressure within the lungs, and the blood oxygen level remains fairly high to about 10,000 feet. To illustrate, the oxygen saturation level of the blood is 97 percent at sea level, 94 percent at 7,000 feet and 90 percent at 10,000 feet. Above this point the saturation falls rapidly to 70 percent at 20,000 feet, 50 percent at 23,000 feet and only about 20 percent at 30,000 feet. Because unconsciousness usually occurs between 25 and 50 percent saturation, mountain climbers are required to use oxygen at altitudes over 20,000 feet if activity is carried on for very long. In order to avoid dizziness, headache, and premature exhaustion, oxygen is often used at altitudes much lower than 20,000 feet.

Fortunately, the physiological systems are capable of making certain adjustments to offset partially the lesser availability of oxygen. The combined effect of these adjustments are immediate but minor in their results, while others take several weeks of living in the higher elevation.

The important point is for backpackers to recognize that oxygen density diminishes with altitude and this has a negative effect on one's ability to do prolonged vigorous exercise. One should not try to fight this problem, but rather recognize its presence and adjust the exercise rate accordingly.

Conserving Energy

In hiking, as in other locomotive activities, stopping, starting, accelerating, and decelerating are costly in terms of energy. The most economical approach is to distribute the available energy evenly by traveling at an even pace. Also keep in mind that much less energy is expended in hiking a given distance over level ground than climbing up and down slopes, so from the standpoint of energy conservation, select a route which is as level as possible. Further, recognize that the faster your pace the more energy you utilize per mile. So don't travel too fast if you want to save energy.

11
Problems Of Hypothermia And Hyperthermia

Everybody needs beauty as well as bread . . . where nature may heal and cheer and give strength to body and soul alike.

Hypothermia and hyperthermia have to do with cold and heat injuries respectively. Fortunately, these conditions occur infrequently to backpackers. But they *are* potential hazards and should not be taken lightly.

Hypothermia

In the middle of September in beautiful weather, five experienced backpackers set out on a four-day journey to the Goat Rock area of Washington. All were well equipped for the trek with food, shelter, clothing, and emergency supplies. On the second day, the trail led high up onto the exposed cliffs. Unexpectedly, as can happen at high altitudes, inclement weather suddenly settled in—first gusty winds, then rain, sleet, and hail. The hikers continued upward, thinking that the storm would subside as quickly as it had started, but it did not. Before long, one member of the party was seen leaning against a rock, shaking violently, and his hands had begun to swell.

> **WHEN HYPOTHERMIA IS A POSSIBILITY, IT'S ESPECIALLY IMPORTANT TO KEEP YOUR BODY COVERED OVER ALL PARTS. AVOID PROLONGED CONTACT WITH ANYTHING COOLER THAN BODY TEMPERATURE AND STAY DRY. HEAT CAN BE LOST THROUGH CONDUCTION, PERSPIRATION, RADIATION, CONVECTION, RESPIRATION, WIND CHILL AND WATER CHILL.**

The party members decided it was time to retreat down the mountain, but they had made the decision too late. As they proceeded downward, a second member succumbed to the harsh weather and collapsed. With two members disabled, and the other three beginning to show signs of exposure, it was decided to leave the two immobilized members and go for help.

The two were placed in an area protected from the wind with foam mattresses for ground insulation while tarps and sleeping bags were used for additional protection from the weather. When the rescuers arrived back at the scene the following day, they found one person dead and the other barely alive.

What had happened? A simple physiological transaction had occurred. Due to lack of attention to weather conditions, the hikers were caught unaware by the storm and promptly lost body heat faster than it was being produced. This process results in the condition known as hypothermia. The more common terminology that means essentially the same is "overexposure to cold."

The risks of hypothermia are greater for the unsuspecting. There are many hunters and backpackers affected every year, but most cases are not serious because they are recognized and treated before real damage results. But, each year several people end up losing their lives because of inadequate knowledge, or lack of preparedness, relative to hypothermia. Don't let one of these victims be you.

Symptoms and Treatment

There are some distinct signs of hypothermia which can cause you to recognize the condition before it becomes serious. Certain of these signs can be observed by the victim himself, while some can be observed by other members of the party. The symptoms are: (a) thickness of speech; (b) irrationality; (c) weakness and slowing of pace; (d) dilation of pupils; (e) pale and bluish tint to the skin and puffiness of the face and hands; (f) intense shivering; (g) loss of coordination, as illustrated by staggering and stumbling; and (h) a feeling of deep cold.

The treatment for hypothermia is much a matter of common sense. But here are some guidelines that will be helpful: (a) immediately provide shelter from wind and cold; (b) be sure the victim's clothing is dry or remove wet clothing and place the victim in warm bedding; (c) increase exercise to produce more body heat—isometric exercises are effective if the victim is not free to move around; and (d) add heat by such means as more clothing or blankets, hot drinks, body-to-body contact or fire. Alcoholic beverages have a negative influence on body heat production, so they should never be consumed by one suffering from hypothermia. If a location is reached where the victim can be immersed in **warm** water, this is an acceptable treatment. But keep in mind that the circulation in the surface areas of the body will be subnormal, therefore the skin will burn and damage easily. The water should be only slightly warmer than normal body temperature (about 100°F.).

Methods of prevention should become second nature to experienced backpackers and the methods should include: (a) sufficient rest at timely intervals; (b) proper nutrition; (c) adequate clothing kept dry by effective preventative measures; (d) sufficient exercise to keep up the body's heat production; and common sense to know when to stop and set up camp or turn back when the conditions justify doing so.

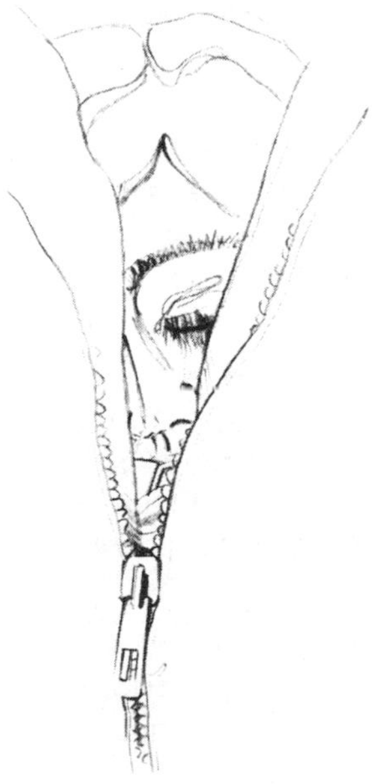

Figure 11-1. For a victim of hypothermia, one or more sleeping bags can be effectively used to help reestablish normal body temperature. Further loss of body heat must be strictly avoided.

Frostbite

Frostbite usually occurs at the extremities or on areas where the skin is exposed. One of the early symptoms is flushing of the skin, then the skin color changes to white or greyish white. Pain is sometimes felt early but subsides later as the area becomes numb. In some areas, such as the cheeks and forehead, there is usually no pain—only a mild stinging sensation prior to numbness. The victim might not be aware of frostbite until someone tells him about his pale, glossy skin. In extreme cases water blisters develop.

By being alert to the symptoms, serious frostbite can be prevented. If a body part becomes cold, place it against a warm body part. The hands can be placed between the thighs or under the arms; the nose can be covered in the bend of the elbow or with the hands, and areas in the face and head can be covered for short periods with the hands, with a hat, a neckerchief, or other material. Physical activity is helpful because it causes additional heating of the body. Exercising of the fingers and toes helps to maintain better circulation in those areas.

The objective of the treatment for frostbite should be to restore the body part to normal temperature as quickly as possible without causing injury to the tissues. If the victim can be moved indoors, the body part can be rewarmed by immersing it in water at near body temperature (about 96°F.) never hot water. If the victim is outdoors, it is helpful to do the following: (a) apply mild pressure against the frozen part with a warm hand or other body part; (b) cover the frozen part with a sufficient amount of warm clothing; and, (c) be sure the victim's total body is sufficiently insulated with coats and blankets to maintain normal body temperature. Once the body part is rewarmed, encourage the patient to exercise the muscles in the injured area. This will help restore normal circulation more quickly.

It is important to handle the frozen part with great care, and **avoid** the following: (a) rubbing the area, because this may damage surface tissue, and increase the risk of tissue death; (b) don't immerse in water hotter than body temperature, because frozen tissue which has insufficient blood circulation is very subject to burning; and (c) don't apply hot water bottles or place the frozen part near a hot stove or fire.

Wind Chill Factor

The **actual** temperature of the air is one consideration, but a more important consideration is the effective temperature, or **wind chill factor.** This is determined by a combination of air temperature and wind velocity, and it can be calculated from the following chart:

Water Chill Factor

The thermal conductivity of water is 32 times greater than that of still air. This means that wet clothing will extract much more heat from the body

Temp-erature (°F)	WIND (miles per hour)								Winds above 40 mph have little additional effect
	5	10	15	20	25	30	35	40	
	Equivalent Chill Temperature								
40	35	30	25	20	15	10	10	10	
35	30	20	15	10	10	5	5	0	**LITTLE**
30	25	15	10	5	0	0	−5	−5	**DANGER**
25	20	10	0	0	−5	−10	−10	−15	
20	15	5	−5	−10	−15	−20	−20	−20	
15	10	0	−10	−15	−20	−25	−30	−30	**INCREASING**
10	5	−10	−20	−25	−30	−30	−35	−35	**DANGER**
5	0	−15	−25	−30	−35	−40	−40	−45	**(flesh may**
0	−5	−20	−30	−35	−45	−50	−50	−55	**freeze**
−5	−10	−25	−40	−45	−50	−55	−60	−60	**within one**
−10	−15	−35	−45	−50	−60	−65	−65	−70	**minute)**
−15	−20	−40	−50	−60	−65	−70	−75	−75	
−20	−25	−45	−60	−65	−75	−80	−80	−85	**GREAT**
−25	−30	−50	−65	−75	−80	−85	−90	−95	**DANGER**
−30	−35	−60	−70	−80	−90	−95	−100	−100	**(flesh may**
−35	−40	−65	−80	−85	−95	−100	−105	−110	**freeze**
−40	−45	−70	−85	−95	−105	−110	−115	−115	**within**
−45	−50	−75	−90	−100	−110	−115	−120	−125	**thirty**
−50	−55	−80	−100	−110	−120	−125	−130	−130	**seconds)**
−55	−60	−90	−105	−115	−125	−130	−135	−140	
−60	−70	−95	−110	−120	−135	−140	−145	−150	

Table 11-1. Temperature and wind chill chart.

than dry clothing. Wool is exceptional in the sense that it retains 40 to 50 percent of its insulating value even when wet. In guarding against the unfortunate condition of wet clothing, keep in mind that clothes not only become wet from rain, snow, and dew, but also from perspiration. Too much perspiring should be avoided, especially under cool and windy conditions. The rate of perspiration can be controlled by properly adjusting the layers of clothing and setting your pace so that you work at a moderate, constant level.

Hyperthermia

Hyperthermia is a label given to the physical problems that develop as a result of overheating of the body through exercise. Overheating is more often associated with distance running and early-season football practices in hot weather. But under hot and humid conditions, backpackers must also be alert to this potential problem.

When the body is exercised for a prolonged period in hot weather, **heat stroke** (or sun stroke) can develop. A related condition known as heat exhaustion can also occur, particularly when the humidity is high.

While attempting to counterbalance body overheating, a person can incur large sweat losses of five to ten percent of body weight. Dehydration of such proportions severely limits subsequent sweating, places dangerous demands on circulation, and reduces exercise capacity.

Because of the hazards associated with long duration heavy exercise under heat stress conditions, the American College of Sports Medicine has given special attention to this topic. Here are some guidelines extracted from their information:

1. Vigorous exercise of long duration should not be conducted when the humidity is high and the temperature exceeds 85°F.
2. When working under heat stress conditions, a person should ingest moderate amounts of fluids often (about every half hour) in order to counteract sweat loss and avoid dehydration.
3. Early recognition of sypmtoms, immediate cessation of exercise and proper treatment can prevent serious heat injury. Early warning symptoms include chilling, throbbing pressure in the head, unsteadiness, nausea, dry skin, and loss of orientation.
4. Under heat stress conditions, wear minimal clothing and clothing which ventilates effectively, and expose a larger amount of skin to the air than usual because this will enhance heat dissipation.

Good physical conditioning has a positive effect on the body's tolerance to heat resulting from exercise. Also, a period of acclimatization to exercise under heat stress conditions is important. The physiological changes which occur as a result of several days of acclimatization are: (a) increased circulatory stability characterized by increased circulating blood volume and a reduction of heart rate; (b) increased sensitivity of the sweat mechanism; (c) increased efficiency of the evaporative cooling; and (d) a prolonged gradual increase in sweat production.

Heat Stroke

The symptoms of this condition are headache, hot dry skin, rapid pulse and unusually high body temperature. In severe cases the temperature might exceed 105°F. Heat stroke is extremely dangerous (life threatening) especially among older people.

The first aid treatment involves immediate cooling of the body, total rest, sufficient disrobing to provide extensive ventilation, and administration of a liquid salt solution as explained under heat exhaustion. Sponge the body freely with rubbing alcohol or lukewarm water to reduce body temperature. Provide medical assistance as soon as possible.

The best indications of recovery are the lowering of body temperature and reduction of pulse rate. As these return close to normal, there is good evidence of improvement but still the victim should be watched carefully for possible relapse.

Dehydration

In order for the body systems to function efficiently during prolonged exercise, the fluids which are utilized or evaporated must be replenished. This is done best by consuming small amounts of fluid frequently so that the body fluid is replenished at about the same rate as it is used. During heavy perspiration, body salt is lost and it should be replenished by taking one salt tablet per day to supplement the normal supply, or by mixing small amounts of salt with the water that is consumed. Severe dehydration is very serious and can result in death.

Heat Cramps

Cramps may occur in the abdominal muscles or the muscles of the legs. This condition is often associated with heat exhaustion and it is caused by the loss of fluids and chemicals from profuse sweating.

Heat cramps usually respond to firm constant pressure applied with the hand directly on the cramped area. The application of warm towels also helps. In addition, complete rest of the body part and the administration of a salt water solution is helpful. If vigorous exercise is anticipated at warm temperatures one salt tablet per day can help avoid heat cramps.

12
Emergency Care And Treatment

Of what value is eternity for a person so devoid of imagination that he's incapable of using even a day of leisure to great advantage.

First aid is exactly what the term implies—it is the treatment given first when a person becomes injured or ill. Normally such treatment is quite basic, but sometimes it is extremely important even to the point of saving a person's life. Fortunately, it is very seldom that a backpacker needs to administer first aid for a serious injury but, on the rare occasions when the need arises, it is obviously important to be prepared. By necessity, the information given in this chapter is brief. It contains only the essential first aid treatments of particular injuries that backpackers are most likely to deal with. It is recommended that every serious backpacker become better prepared by completing an American National Red Cross first aid course. Information about the places and times that the course is taught can be obtained from the local Red Cross office.

The most serious injuries with which first aiders must deal include serious bleeding, traumatic shock, food poisoning, cessation of breathing, and blows to the head. In the absence of proper first aid treatment, all of these conditions can result in death.

Figure 12-1. A knife is a handy tool for a backpacker.

In the case of serious injuries, one important aspect of treatment is to keep the individual calm, comfortable, and warm while the necessary medical assistance is obtained as quickly as possible. It's important to be encouraging to the victim and strictly avoid making statements about the injury or circumstance that might cause the victim additional concern or worry. Remember, too much treatment by a first aider can sometimes cause more harm than good. Some first aid procedures are little more than the application of common sense.

The most important single concept in first aid is "prevention is better than cure." This should be kept foremost in mind and practiced to its fullest. One aspect of prevention is being sensitive to situations that might result in injury or illness and making honest efforts to avoid them.

First Aid Kit

A backpacker's first aid kit should be well planned to contain the essential items in contact form. A list of items that can be packed into a small container includes:

- Wide adhesive tape. This has many uses, from taping a sprained ankle to fixing a broken pack frame.
- Bandaids of assorted sizes—three or four of each.
- Sterile gauze squares—2 in. x 3 in.
- A 3-inch ace bandage.
- A large neckerchief.
- A dozen small safety pins.
- Needle, thread, tweezers, and single-edged razor blade.
- Chapstick and sunscreen (zinc oxide, pre-sun or scolex are recommended).
- Insect repellent (cutter cream is recommended).
- Aspirin for headaches and pain.
- Antiseptic.
- Water purifier.
- Salt tablets.
- Snake bite kit (optional depending on the area).

THE BASIC SNAKEBIT KIT CONTAINS DISINFECTANT, A SHARP BLADE FOR MAKING INCISIONS, A SET OF SUCTION CUPS, AND A TOURNIQUET. READ THE PRINTED INSTRUCTIONS CAREFULLY AND UNDERSTAND THEM COMPLETELY BEFORE ANY EMERGENCY ARISES.

Blisters

Blisters usually result from friction caused by a poorly fitted boot, a foreign object in the shoe, or a wrinkle or hole in a sock. A small blister can usually be protected so that it can heal without breaking, and this is the best procedure to follow. Larger blisters that are in locations where they will likely become broken should be drained. This is done best with the use of a needle which has been sterilized by holding the point in the flame of a match for a few seconds. The needle is inserted through the skin at the base of the blister, then the fluid is drained by applying gentle pressure to the blister. A sterile bandage should be applied.

> **TO GUARD AGAINST BLISTERS, APPLY A LARGE PIECE OF MOLESKIN OR MOLEFOAM BEFORE STARTING TO HIKE OR AS SOON AS YOU FEEL A "HOT SPOT." TRIM THE CORNERS TO PREVENT THE DRESSING FROM PEELING OFF.**

If a blister develops in a location where it causes pain while walking, or if walking will cause additional damage to the blister, a ridge should be built around the blister to prevent direct pressure upon it. This can be done with a thin layer of sponge rubber or felt cut into a doughnut shape and taped over the blister. Also it can be accomplished by using several layers of tape.

Most potential blisters can be **prevented** by following sound procedures, keeping in mind that proper footwear is among a backpacker's most important equipment. Proper treatment of early symptoms will usually prevent the blister from developing.

Altitude Sickness

When a person ascends rapidly to high altitude, the physiological systems must adjust to the new environment. The thinner air causes more rapid breathing, plus other adjustments in the oxygen delivery system. In some regions where climbers frequently ascend from near sea level to elevations of over 10,000 feet in one day (partly by motor vehicle), altitude sickness occurs frequently. The symptoms include: (a) headache; (b) nausea; (c) uncontrollable tendency to sleep; and (d) shortness of breath during exertion. Prevention and treatment include frequent rest stops, movement at a gradual and even pace between rest stops, deep breathing, nourishment from quick energy foods, and movement to a lower altitude until symptoms disappear. Aspirin can be taken if needed for headaches.

Traumatic Shock

Shock is a depressed condition of the body's functions due to loss of blood or severe pain resulting from injury. Emotional stress can also be a contributing factor. Shock is almost always associated with severe burns, wounds, or fractures. Traumatic shock can be fatal.

139

The most apparent symptom is weakness, while other symptoms are vacant and lack-luster eyes with dilated pupils; shallow and irregular breathing; weak and rapid pulse; pale, cold, moist skin; and nausea.

The treatment for shock includes: (a) keeping the patient in the reclining position to ensure an adequate flow of blood to the head and chest; and (b) keeping him warm but not hot. The victim will ordinarily chill due to insufficient circulation. Warmth can be accomplished best by wrapping the victim loosely in blankets. It is better that the patient be slightly cool than too warm.

The victim will usually crave fluid and have an honest physiological need for it. If medical assistance can be reached within a half hour the giving of fluid by the first-aider is not very important. However, if assistance is a long way off, the victim should be given small amounts of warm water at short intervals, about a half a glass at a time unless unconscious or only partially conscious, in which case fluid should not be given.

It is important to control the causes of shock as much as possible; bleeding should be stopped, pain should be reduced, and the victim should be relieved of emotional stress.

Open Wounds

In treating open wounds, there are two primary considerations: (a) control the bleeding; and (b) prevent contamination. In addition, if the wound is severe and painful, treatment for shock is an important consideration.

Almost all bleeding can be controlled by direct pressure over the wound. To accomplish this, apply a sterile gauze pad directly over the wound, cover it with the cleanest available cloth, and apply constant firm pressure for 10 to 15 minutes. As long as bleeding continues, the risk of infection is negligible compared to the risk from blood loss.

If direct pressure is not successful, then the application of pressure at one of the arterial pressure points might be effective. The tourniquet is the very last resort, but in rare instances it may be necessary in order to save the victim's life. In the case of the loss of a limb, a tourniquet is necessary.

To prevent contamination, touch the wound only with clean and sterile material. After bleeding has stopped, the wound should be washed clean with soap and water. The application of a mild antiseptic is optional. Then bandage the wound with a sterile bandage. If the wound is deep and small, making it difficult to clean thoroughly, infection is an important concern. In such cases, medical assistance should be obtained. If the wound involves a large opening, a bandage should be applied in a manner that closes the wound as much as possible in order to avoid a large scar.

Sprains

A sprain in a joint occurs when force causes movement beyond the normal range of motion, thus causing damage to the connective tissues that cross over the joint. In addition, small blood vessels are usually ruptured and this results in discoloration. Swelling, pain and tenderness are the immediate symptoms.

The treatment consists of: (a) application of either wet or dry cold during the first half-hour to keep down the swelling; (b) elevation of the sprained part during the first half-hour or longer; and (c) partial or total immobilization of the joint. An ace bandage or elastic bandage can be wrapped snugly around the sprained part to keep the swelling down and contribute to immobilization. If it appears there is a possibility of a fracture, it is best to treat the injury as if a fracture exists.

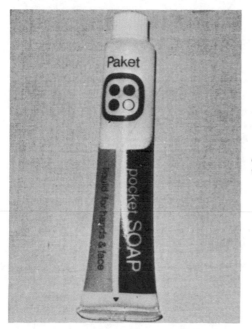

Figure 12-2. A small tube of liquid soap can serve an excellent cleansing purpose in the first aid treatment of open wounds.

Fractures

There are two principal kinds of bone fractures; **simple** and **compound.** A simple fracture is when the broken bone does not protrude through the skin, whereas a compound fracture involves an open wound caused by the broken bone.

A fracture is easy to identify when the bones are displaced. When this condition is not present, the fracture is more difficult to recognize. An important guide is that if you suspect a fracture, treat the victim as if the fracture does exist. In addition to deformity, other important symptoms are: tenderness when direct pressure is applied; pain, especially when associated with motion; and swelling. Often it is helpful to have an explanation of what happened along with the victim's evaluation of his or her condition.

The important aspects of first aid are: (a) protect the broken bone from any movement (immobilize it) because motion may cause additional damage to the broken ends and to surrounding tissue, and it will cause pain; (b) treat for shock; and (c) in the case of a compound fracture treat the open wound.

Body parts can be immobilized by different methods, one of which is splinting. Immobilization might also be accomplished with a traction device, or by wrapping the area with several layers of newspaper or several layers of blanket. The victim should be moved as little as possible and only with great care, keeping in mind the possibility of further injury.

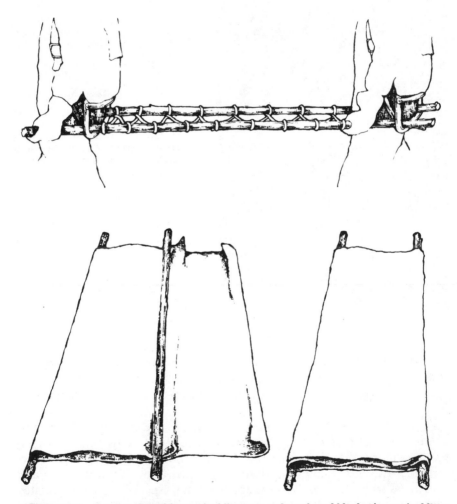

Figure 12-3. A pole and rope improvised litter top and a pole and blanket improvised litter (a sleeping bag can be used in the place of a blanket).

Dislocations

A dislocation of a joint is where the head of the bone becomes displaced from the socket. Joints where this is the most apt to happen are the shoulder, wrist, and fingers. Serious dislocations should be treated essentially the same as fractures so refer to the explanation in that section. Shock is an important consideration.

Insect Bites

At certain times of the year, there are insects which bite, sting, and thoroughly frustrate backpackers. It is a very good idea to find out before departure what kinds of troublesome insects are in season and how to cope with them.

The **mosquito** is often the greatest pest during the summer months, and there are three kinds of preventive measures to consider: (a) clothing that covers the arms, hands, legs, neck, and head; (b) insect repellent; and (c) netting for the head.

An adequate supply of insect repellent should always be part of a backpacker's supplies. The main ingredient of all effective mosquito repellents is the same, N - Diethyl - Metatolnamide. The proportion of this compound varies from brand to brand. Cutter cream is considered the most effective and it is the most compact, but there are several brands containing the above compound which are effective for repelling mosquitos. Also, the juice from wild onion or garlic is fairly effective for repelling insects (and people).

Mosquito bites ordinarily do not require treatment, but sometimes it is comforting to apply calamine lotion, rubbing alcohol, or some form of cream to ease the itching. However, these substances have no healing effects.

If a **tick** gets on your body but has not yet burrowed into the skin it can be gently removed. However, if the tick has broken through the surface and is firmly attached, the two best methods of removal are: (1) cover the area with a heavy oil thus closing off all oxygen to the tick and allow a few minutes for it to suffocate or remove itself; or (2) place a sterilized needle just under the skin above the tick's head and flip the needle upward. Another method though less effective is to touch the tick with the tip of a hot needle. This will cause it to loosen its grip. If a tick which is firmly attached is simply pulled away, the body will often break off and leave the tick's head in the skin. After the tick has been completely removed, the area should be thoroughly covered with an antiseptic.

Most **stings** are not very serious and they usually involve only temporary pain and local swelling. The best treatment is to remove the stinger if it is left in the skin by scraping the stinger off with a sharp edge of a knife or razor blade. Tweezers can also be used but this sometimes squeezes addi-

Figure 12-4. A sharp knife can be used effectively in removing a stinger from the flesh.

tional poison from the poison sack. Then apply cold packs or emerse the area in cold water. This slows swelling and eases pain. Also it is helpful to apply mud over the sting. This has a cooling effect and as the mud dries it draws out some of the poison.

Chiggers are small, flea-like insects found in the moist eastern and southern sectors of the United States. Their bites are not serious but can be irritating. Prevention amounts to keeping the body, particularly the legs, well covered with clothing and adequate application of insect repellent. Treatment is the same as explained for mosquito bites.

Spider and Scorpion Bites

The **black widow spider** is often considered an inhabitant of domestic areas but it can be found almost anyplace within its geographic region—under rocks, in abandoned animal holes, or hollow logs. The female, which is larger and more dangerous than the male, is shiny black with a bright red hour glass on the abdomen. The smaller male is light brown with vertical stripes and he has a less obvious spot on his abdomen.

A person will not likely die from a black widow bite, although it is possible; but a bite can cause severe discomfort. A result will be a small amount of redness and swelling at the location of the bite and rather severe pain throughout the musculature of the body. The victim will experience extensive sweating and possibly nausea, difficulty in breathing, and abdominal cramps. If the bite is on a finger or toe, immediately apply a tight constriction band at the base of the finger or toe. If the bite is on the arm or leg, apply a broader restriction band above the bite but remove it after a maximum of ten minutes. Keep the area as low as possible in order to retard flow of blood back to the heart. Apply cold water or cold packs to the bitten area for one and a half to two hours and seek the aid of a physician immediately.

The **tarantula** has been dramatized as a horrible creature capable of striking almost immediate death, but actually most species of the tarantula have a bite of about the same severity as a wasp sting. There are species outside of the United States that are highly poisonous, but none of these are native to this country. In order to be safe and comforting to the victim, treat a tarantula bite the same as a black widow bite.

Scorpions are encountered rather frequently by outdoorsmen in the warm or desert regions. They like cool damp spots such as underneath rocks. In scorpion areas it's especially important to check inside boots and underneath clothing before getting dressed each morning.

Most scorpion stings have about the same effect as a wasp bite, but there are a few that carry enough poison to be highly dangerous even to the point of causing death in a child or an adult who is aged or physically weak. But even a strong adult will experience temporary sickness and discomfort from the sting of a poisonous variety. The symptoms are essentially the same as for the black widow spider and the treatment is also the same.

Snake Bites

Bites by poisonous snakes can usually be avoided by exercising a reasonable level of caution but ocassionally someone will get bitten and, when this happens, it should be considered an emergency. The treatment should be aimed at: (a) removal of as much venom as possible; (b) retarding absorption of the venom; (c) neutralizing the venom; (d) treatment of the damage done to the flesh by both the bite and the first aid procedure; and (e) treatment for potential shock.

An attempt should be made immediately to identify whether the snake is venomous. If it is identified as a rattlesnake, coral snake, copperhead, or watermouth moccasin, it is poisonous. Bites by non-poisonous snakes are frightening, but not dangerous. If fang marks are present, you know the snake is poisonous and the danger is significant. A burning sensation, swelling, and redness around the wound, are signs of poisoning.

The treatment should be quick and it consists of (a) applying a constriction band, (b) cutting small incision, (c) suction of venom, and (d) rest. Keep the victim as calm and composed as possible.

If the bite is on a limb such as the arm or leg, a **flat** tourniquet such as a belt should be applied between the bite and the heart. Tighten it only to the point that a finger can still be put underneath. This is to block surface veinous return while not seriously hindering deep arterial supply to the limb. Once the tourniquet is in place **do not remove,** although it can be loosened as swelling occurs.

A straight incision through the fang marks **1/4 inch** deep should be made (no cross hatches). Suction of some type can then be applied to the wound. Oral suction should be avoided especially by a person with a cut or sore on the lips or in the mouth. The person should rest in a horizontal position (do not have the injured limb above the level of the heart). If anti-venom is available and someone is qualified in its use, it should be administered.

After the treatment for the bite itself has been completed, the incision should be treated in the same manner as other open wounds. Cool packs over the wound will reduce the swelling. The limb should be immobilized and the victim should receive rest and encouragement. He should be evacuated by litter or motor vehicle as quickly as possible and placed under medical care.

Traumatic shock is a possibility and, if it occurs, can be more serious than the bite itself so watch for symptoms of shock and treat accordingly. (See section on shock.)

In the near future there probably will be on the market a snakebite vaccine which can be given to provide immunity for all poisonous snakebites. One who spends much time in the out of doors will certainly want to look into this.

Animal Bites

In addition to treatment of the wound itself, the danger from animal bites is infection and the possibility of rabies. The bite should be washed thoroughly with soap and water and a sterile dressing applied.

Many animals are capable of carrying rabies. Therefore, when possible, the animal inflicting the bite should be captured or killed and the head should be preserved so that the brain can undergo laboratory tests. Rabies is a very serious disease and treatment for potential rabies should begin as quickly as medical assistance can be acquired.

Plant Poisoning

Stinging nettle, poison ivy, oak and sumac are pesty plants which cause irritations when touched directly against the skin. An experienced hiker can usually avoid these plants by knowing how to identify them and being cautious. Once it is known that contact has been made, the skin should be washed immediately with soap and water. This will remove most of the substance which causes skin irritation. Do not scrub with a brush because this will work the substance deeper into the pores. The use of a cortisone skin cream will soothe and relieve the itching, as will calamine lotion, rubbing alcohol or a mild face cream.

Nosebleeds

Nosebleeds are not uncommon among outdoorsmen, especially at high altitudes. They are usually not serious, just pesty. A nosebleed can usually be controlled by one or a combination of the following—(a)sit down, let the head hang as low as possible between the knees, and apply mild pressure on the two sides of the nostrils, or (b) assume a reclining position with the chest high and the head tilted backwards, apply cold packs to the nose area. Sometimes stuffing the bleeding nostril with gauze is also effective.

Thermal Burns

Burns are classified according to depth or degree: **first degree**—the skin is reddened; **second degree**—blisters develop on the skin; **third degree**—there is destruction of tissue underneath the skin. The degree of the burn and the amount of body area covered are the two important considerations.

The objectives in emergency treatment of burns are to: (a) relieve pain; (b) prevent contamination; and (c) treat for traumatic shock. **Shock** is a major consideration when the burn involves more than 10 percent of the body's surface, and sometimes when the area is smaller. Most deaths of burn victims are actually caused by shock. Treatment for shock is discussed in another section of this chapter.

If the burn is relatively minor, the pain can be relieved by applying cool water or a cold pack for about 15 minutes; then apply burn ointment or petroleum jelly and wrap the burn with a sterile dressing. In the case of a severe burn, apply a sterile dressing to protect the burn from the air and give the victim aspirin to further relieve the pain. Then treat for shock and obtain medical assistance as quickly as possible.

Deep burns are very subject to infection; therefore, avoiding **contamination** is very important. Clean hands and clean dressings are essential.

For a burn of the **eye**, irritate the eye gently, causing it to water. This will protect the eye from the air, and help remove foreign materials. Bathing the eye with clean, pure water is also helpful. Close the eyelid, cover the eye with a clean bandage or cloth, and immediately seek medical aid.

Sunburn

Severe **sunburn** is essentially the same as a thermal burn and should be treated accordingly. Prevention of sunburn is much easier and less painful than treatment, and sunburn can and should be avoided. Protective clothing and sun screen or lotion ought to be used as needed.

Muscle Cramp

Occasionally someone who has hiked and climbed vigorously for several hours will suffer cramps in muscles of the legs or abdomen. This may be due to loss of salt through perspiration, or from a build-up of lactic acid in the muscles. The best prevention is to use an even and reasonable pace, and supplement the usual diet with one or two salt tablets daily.

First aid treatment involves: (a) applying direct constant pressure on the muscle; (b) slowly stretching the cramped muscle and holding it on stretch; (c) relaxation of the muscle to permit the lactic acid build-up to be removed faster; and (d) one or two salt tablets.

Water Purification

The best method of purifying water is with Halazone tablets, which are available in almost all sporting good stores. Recognize that these tablets are dated so be sure the tablets you have are still usable. Just follow the instructions on the container. Another method is to add four drops of chlorine (or Purex which is almost 100 percent chlorine) to each pint of water. This will dispose of any bacteria that might be in the water. Boiling the water before use is another method of purification that works effectively, but it is often less convenient than purification.

Artificial Respiration

Artificial respiration might be needed in connection with a number of conditions such as; heart attack, traumatic shock, near drowning, or suffocation. The most effective method is mouth-to-mouth resuscitation. Following are the steps in administering this method:

● Place the victim on the back in a stretched-out and relaxed position. Tilt the head back so the chin is pointing upward and pull the jaw down so the mouth is open. Be sure the mouth and air passage are clear of any obstacles, including the tongue.

Figure 12-5. Mouth-to-mouth resuscitation: correctly position the victim's upper body and head (top), then blow air into the victim's mouth while closing the nasal passage with your cheek or free hand.

● Open your mouth wide and place it tightly over the victim's mouth, and at the same time pinch the victim's nostrils shut, or close the nostrils with your cheek pressed against them. Then blow air into the victim's lungs. (If there is special reason to do so, you can hold the mouth closed and blow air through the victim's nose.)

● Remove your mouth, turn your head to the side and listen for the rush of exhaled air.

● Repeat the procedure at the rate of 12 to 15 times per minute for adults or about 20 times per minute for children, using more shallow breaths.

Injuries Related to Cold and Heat

The previous chapter on hypothermia and hyperthermia explains how to deal with overexposure to cold and frostbite as well as such heat injuries as heat exhaustion, heat stroke, heat cramps, and dehydration. These treacherous injuries can usually be avoided by good judgment and reasonable precautions. Both prevention and care are discussed in the previous chapter.

13
Which Items To Take

The quality of the environment, like freedom and justice, must be protected and achieved anew by each generation.

This section includes two kinds of information: (1) explanation of items that are essential on backpacking trips and items which are convenient but not always necessary; and (2) a check-list of all the items that should be considered for any particular trip.

Essentials

In addition to the standard supplies and equipment discussed in previous sections under food, cooking equipment, sleeping gear, shelters, and clothing, the following items ought to always be taken.

Matches and Fire Starter. Even if you don't plan to make a fire, you should always be prepared to do so in case of emergency. It is recommended that you have an adequate supply of stick matches packed in two separate waterproof containers. The second container is a safety measure in case the first container becomes lost or its contents depleted. The reason for waterproof containers is obvious to experienced outdoorsmen. "Fire starter," which can be purchased in most sporting good stores, or a two-inch section of candle would prove very useful in starting a fire. In addition, the candle can be used to furnish light if needed.

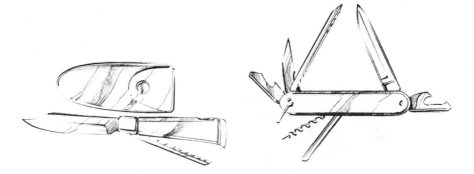

Figure 13-1. Two varities of useful knives for the backpacker: a belt knife (left) and a multiple use pocket knife (right).

Knife. A good knife is invaluable to a backpacker. A high-quality versatile pocket knife is usually preferred over a hunting knife. One of the best pocket knives is the true Swiss Army Knife which includes high quality steel blades, screw driver, hole punch, scissors, tweezers, can opener, etc. It's a good idea to keep your knife fastened to the pack or to your belt with a shoelace or strip of rawhide.

First Aid Supplies. A basic first aid kit can be made very compact for backpacking use. The content of such a kit is described at the beginning of Chapter 13.

Flashlight. The best kind of flashlight is a very compact one which uses two "D" batteries. It is easy to carry and can serve as a dependable source of light under various conditions.

Canteen. Because water is usually not available at all points along the hiking trail, and since sometimes you cannot depend on the purity of the water, a canteen is useful to get you from one suitable waterhole to the next. Consider only a light canteen made of either plastic or aluminum with a good quality lid.

Compass and Map. A reliable compass and accurate map should always be carried unless you're in an area with which you are highly familiar. The use of the map and compass is explained in the section on Routes and Navigation.

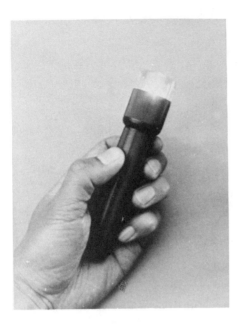

Figure 13-2. A flashlight—"the last light": virtually indestructable and at the same time, small and lightweight.

Extra Clothing. The weather is always somewhat unpredictable and so are the other circumstances with which you might be confronted. Therefore, it is important to have the necessary extra items of clothing to protect you against possible adverse weather or a possible delayed return. An extra pair of socks, an extra sweater and a lightweight poncho or sheet of plastic are useful items that should be taken along.

Extra Food. An extra one day supply of dehydrated food weighs only about two pounds. One or more packages ought to be carried as a safety measure. Bad weather, or any number of things, may extend a backpacking trip and along with these unforseeable events comes the need for more food.

Optionals

The optional items are closely related to one's preference. A list of the optional items that almost every backpacker should consider includes:

Sunglasses. In most backpacking areas, one can get by nicely without sunglasses, but they are an important convenience. Some people consider them so important that they carry an extra pair in the pack in case the first pair becomes broken or lost.

Nylon Cord. A twenty-foot length of lightweight nylon cord has many uses, such as tying items to the pack, repairing packs and pack frames, construction of shelters, the hanging of items from trees, etc. It uses up very little space and adds very little weight.

Insect Repellent. If there is any chance that repellent will be needed, it should certainly be included in the pack. Liquid uses much less space than sprays.

Skin Care Substances. The need for this is influenced by one's complexion and skin condition, and climatic conditions. Consider the effects of sun exposure, wind and soil and have the substances with you that are necessary to take good care of your skin. Suntan cream and chapstick are two important skin care items.

Watch. Although many people consider a watch to be an essential, it really is not. In fact, some backpackers choose not to have one because the constant presence of a clock is one of the modern conveniences they want to avoid. There certainly are some advantages to having a watch, but some prefer to forego the advantages in order to create a timeless, back to nature effect.

Camera and Film. Many believe there is no better way to remember a trip than through photographs, and photography is certainly a wonderful hobby which is compatible with backpacking. If you carry camera equipment, keep it in a plastic bag for protection. Water can quickly ruin both camera and film.

Fishing Equipment. Fishing is one of the prime motivators of many backpackers. Fortunately, there are compact fishing reels and poles which collapse to about 12 inches in length. Combined with a small box of well selected fishing accessories, these items add much interest and excitement to backpacking trips in areas where fishing is good.

Books and Games. You may not think that a book or small table game has any place on backpacking trips, but if you've ever been cooped up in a tent for a day or two because of weather, you know that something to pass the time can seem very important. A miniature deck of cards weighs less than two ounces and compact chess sets are available. Also, a good paperback book would go a long way toward adding interest to a day in a tent.

Equipment Checklist

For a one-day trip that does not involve overnight camping, only certain items need to be selected from the following list:

- Clothing, suitable footwear, heavy soft socks, tough trousers that are wind repellent with belt, comfortable underwear, long sleeved shirt, sweater, light parka or windbreaker, hat or cap, light gloves (optional), extra socks (optional)
- Sunglasses, suntan lotion, and chapstick
- Watch
- Map and Compass (optional)
- Lunch and trail snacks
- Small first aid kit

Figure 13-3. A lightweight grill for backpackers offers a convenient tool for frying foods.

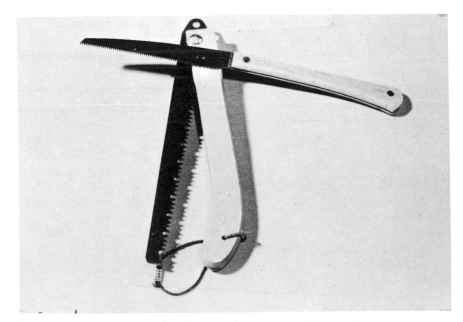

Figure 13-4. Two types of small folding saws that take very little space in backpack.

- Nylon cord (optional)
- Poncho (optional)
- Knife (multi-item pocketknife is recommended)
- Canteen and water purification tablets
- Matches
- Flashlight

For an **overnight trip** (or several nights) the following items should be seriously considered:

- All of the items listed under Day Trips
- Additional clothing as needed for the cool nights and additional days
- Candle (large diameter) for light and fire starting
- Food (plan the menu thoroughly and package the food by meals)
- Cooking and eating utensils (carry the minimum needed depending upon your menu and your outdoor living style)
- Campstove
- Extra fuel
- Tent (optional)
- Tent Poles and pegs (optional)
- Sleeping Pad (optional but recommended)
- Sleeping bag
- Liquid soap
- Selected toilet articles
- Folding saw or hatchet
- Camera and film (optional)
- Pajamas and nightcap (optional)
- Compact sewing and repair kit
- Can opener
- Pencil and note

Appendix A:
Selected Bibliography

Books

Backpacking: One Step at a Time, Harvey Manning (Seattle, REI Press, 1972).

Medicine for Mountaineering, James A. Wilkerson, M.D., ed. (Seattle, The Mountaineers, 1969).

Mountaineering: Freedom of the Hills, Peggy Ferber, ed. (Seattle, The Mountaineers, 1977).

The New Complete Walker, Colin Fletcher (New York, Knopf, 1974).

Outdoor Survival Skills, Larry Dean Olson (Provo, Brigham Young University Press, 1973).

Pathfinder: A Backpacker's Guide, by Don Shaw and Katherine Chaney, (North Palm Beach, Florida, The Athletic Institute, 1980).

Roughing It Easy, Dian Thomas (Provo, Brigham Young University Press, 1974).

Sports Illustrated Backpacking, Michael Sandi (New York, J.B. Lippincott Co., 1980).

Periodicals

Backpacker, Backpacker, Inc., William Kensley, 65 Adams Street, Bedford Hills, NY 10507, 1973.

Wilderness Camping, Fitzgerald Communications, Inc., 1597 Union Street, Schenectady, NY 12309, 1978.

Hiker's Guide, published by National Campers and Hikers Association, Inc., 7172 Transit Road, Buffalo, NY 14221.

Camping Magazine, published by American Camping Association, Bradford Woods, Martinville, IN 46151.

Appendix B:
National Organizations

There are several national organizations which are closely aligned with activities such as backpacking. Each of the organizations has available certain publications and other information of potential interest to outdoor enthusiasts. Some of these organizations also have regional and state offices, the addresses of which can be obtained from the national office.

American Hiking Society, 317 Pennsylvania Avenue, S.E., Washington, D.C. 20003 (has available a trail information packet of each state.

American Youth Hostels, Inc., National Campus, Delaplane, VA 22025 (provides information about hiking and bicycling).

Appalachian Trail Conference, Inc., P.O. Box 236, Harpers Ferry, WV 25425

American Camping Association, Bradford Woods, Martinville, IN 46151 (publishes camping magazine eight times a year).

National Audubon Society, 950 Third Avenue, New York, NY 10022 (publishes Audubon magazine bi-monthly).

National Campers and Hikers Association, Inc. 7172 Transit Road, Buffalo, NY 14221 (publishes a monthly magazine titled Camping Guide).

National Trails Council, P.O. Box 1042, St. Charles, IL 60174.

Sierra Club, 220 Bush Street, San Francisco, CA 94104.

Wilderness Society, 1901 Pennsylvania Avenue, Washington D.C. 20006.

International Backpackers Association, Inc., P.O. Box 85, Lincoln Center, NE 04458.

Appendix C: Government Sources of Information

Each state has an outdoor recreation liaison office which, among other things, is responsible for preparing and implementing the state outdoor recreation plan. This office serves as the focal point for all kinds of outdoor recreation information within the state to include a list of trails, camping areas and regulations for their use, etc.

Also, information and maps for each area of the country can be obtained from regional and local offices of the U.S. Forest Service, the National Park Service, the Bureau of Land Management, and the U.S. Geological Survey.

Appendix D: National Trail System

Under the National Trails Act of 1968, seven national trails have been established. The following is a list of these together with the best source of information about each one:

- Appalachian National Scenic Trail—Appalachian Trail Project Office. National Park Service, P.O. Box 236, Harpers Ferry, WV 25425.

- Pacific Crest National Scenic Trail—Pacific Northwest Regional Office, U.S. Forest Service, 319 S.W. Pine Street, Portland, OR 97208.

- Continental Divide National Scenic Trail—Rocky Mountain Regional Office, U.S. Forest Service, 11177 West Eighth Street, P.O. Box 25127, Lakewood, CO 80225.

- Iditarod National Historic Trail—Anchorage District, Bureau of Land Management, 4700 East 77nd Avenue, Anchorage, AL 99507.

- Oregon National Historic Trail—Pacific Northwest Regional Office, National Park Service, Room 931, 4th and Pike Bldg. 1424 Fourth Avenue, Seattle, WA 98101.

- Lewis and Clark National Historic Trail—Midwest Regional Office, National Park Service, 1709 Jackson Street, Omaha, NE 68102.

- Mormon Pioneer National Historic Trail—Rocky Mountain Regional Office, National Park Service, P.O. Box 25287, Denver, CO 80225.

Appendix E:
Equipment Suppliers

The following is a partial list of the names and addresses of some of the better known outdoor equipment suppliers. Most will furnish a free catalog upon request.

- Adventure 16, Inc.
  4620 Alvarado Canyon Road
  San Diego, CA 92120
  (714) 283-2374

- Camp Trails Company
  4111 W. Clarendon Avenue
  Phoenix, AZ 85019
  (602) 272-9401

- Co-op Wilderness Supply
  1607 Shattuck Avenue
  Berkeley, CA 94709
  (415) 843-9300

- Don Gleason's Campers Supply, Inc.
  9 Pearl St., P.O. Box 87
  Northhampton, MA 01060
  (413) 584-4895

- Early Winters, Ltd.
  110 Prefontaine Place So.
  Seattle, WA 98104
  (206) 622-5203

- Eastern Mountain Sports, Inc.
  6209 Vose Farm Road
  Peterborough, NH 03458
  (603) 924-7276

- Eddie Bauer
  Third & Virginia
  Seattle, WA 98124
  (206) 885-3330

- Frostline Kits
  Frostline Circle
  Denver, CO 80241

- Holubar Mountaineering, Ltd.
  Box 7
  Boulder, CO 80306
  (800) 525-2540 toll-free

- JanSport
  Paine Field Industrial Park
  Everett, WA 98204

- Kelty
  1801 Victory Blvd.
  Glendale, CA 91201

- L.L. Bean, Inc.
  3851 Birch St.
  Freeport, ME 04033
  (207) 865-3111

- Marmot Mountain Works, Ltd.
  331 South 13th
  Grand Junction, CO 81501

- Moor & Mountain
  63 Park St.
  Andover, MA 01810
  (617) 475-3665

- The North Face
  P.O. Box 2399, Station A
  Berkeley, CA 94702
  (415) 525-2026

- P & S Sales
  3818 South 79th East Ave.
  Tulsa, OK 74145

- Recreational Equipment, Inc.
  P.O. Box 88125
  Seattle, WA 98188
  (800) 426-4840 toll-free

- Rivendell Mountain Works
  P.O. Box 199
  Victor, ID 83455

- The Ski Hut
  1615 University Ave.
  Berkeley, CA 94701
  (415) 843-8170

- Wilderness Experience
  20120 Plummer St.
  Chatsworth, CA 91311

- Coleman Company
  250 No. St. Francis Street
  Wichita, KS 67201

- Himalayan Industries
  P.O. Box 950
  Monterey, CA 93940

- Recreational Equipment
  523 Pike Street
  Seattle, WA 98101

- Utica Duxbak Corp.
  Utica, NY 13502

ABOUT THE AUTHORS

CLAYNE R. JENSEN

Clayne Jensen holds a Bachelors and a Masters degree from the University of Utah and a Doctorate degree from Indiana University. He is currently Dean of the College of Health, Physical Education, Recreation and Athletics at Brigham Young University. He has participated extensively in professional organizations, workshops and conferences, many of which pertain to outdoor activities. Further, he has established himself as one of the most prolific writers in his field, having authored or co-authored 13 books which are currently in print and a large number of professional articles. He has received several achievement awards and has been listed in 12 national and international biographical sources, including *Who's Who in Education, Who's Who in the West, International Bibliographies,* and *Men of Achievement.* He has long been an avid outdoorsman, and has contributed significantly through writing and teaching about outdoor subjects.

CRAIG JENSEN

Craig Jensen has had extensive experience in a variety of outdoor activities during all seasons of the year and in various geographic areas. Hunting, fishing, canoeing, skiing and camping have become important aspects of his lifestyle. Being an outstanding student and a former college and profession athlete, he is now a medical student at the University of Utah. His practical experience and specialized knowledge about the structure and capabilities of the body and the functioning of its systems have been especially useful in the content of this book.